Sunset Ideas for
Landscaping
& Garden Remodeling

By the Editors of Sunset Books
and Sunset Magazine

Lane Publishing Co. • Menlo Park, California

Acknowledgments

Sunset Ideas for Landscaping and Garden Remodeling is the very latest in a continuing line of Sunset landscaping books that go back as far as 1950. As was true with earlier editions, this book features the creative work of landscape architects and designers from many regions.

For his valuable consulting help, we offer special thanks to Roy Rydell of Santa Cruz, California.

We are also grateful to the following professionals who gave freely of their help and advice: Theodore Brickman, James M. Chadwick, Barbara G. Cunningham, Chandler D. Fairbank, Guy S. Greene, Fred Lang, Lee Sharfman, Ken Wood, and the Western Wood Products Association.

Edited by Robert G. Bander

Design: Norman S. Gordon

Illustrations: Joe Seney, E. D. Bills

Cover: Container-lined steps enliven this garden scene with color splash of reds, blues, yellows, grays. (See page 32.)
Garden design: R. David Adams. Photographed by Glenn Christiansen.
Title page: Detached deck serves as secluded outdoor studio for young artist.
Garden design: Edward Hume. Photographed by Richard Fish.

Editor, Sunset Books: David E. Clark

Contents

Water steps provide fountainlike drainage down hillside during storms, serve as stairs for climbing, descending hill during more frequent dry spells.

1. Planning the

Native plants flourish on the hillsides above and below this comfortable garden. Hillside at left leads to gazebo; behind swinging seat is carport wall. Design: Donald Estep.

garden you want

Designing with a purpose:
nine ways to go

Privacy *is complete along the winding paths of this parklike native plant garden. Design: Robert W. Chittock.*

Entertaining *on two levels: informality on raised deck, sit-down supper on patio below. Design: Berry Rife.*

Comfort *abounds in patio spa sheltered under arbor with climbing blood-red trumpet vine. Design: Lang & Wood.*

Beautification *from orange and yellow gazanias, multiple-trunked palo verde tree, container-planted octopus agave. Design: Warren Jones*

Flexibility *comes from garden workbench with storage drawers backing condominium entryway. Design: Lang & Wood.*

Ease of maintenance *along walkway with hedge of Indica azalea pruned low, ficus vine on house wall.*

Recreation *explodes with paddle tennis, basketball, handball on small, multiple-use court. Design: Walt Young.*

Safety and convenience *are provided by recessed lights illuminating garden stairs. Design: Roy Rydell.*

Food production *on a gentle slope with vegetables grown in staggered planters. Design: Robert W. Chittock.*

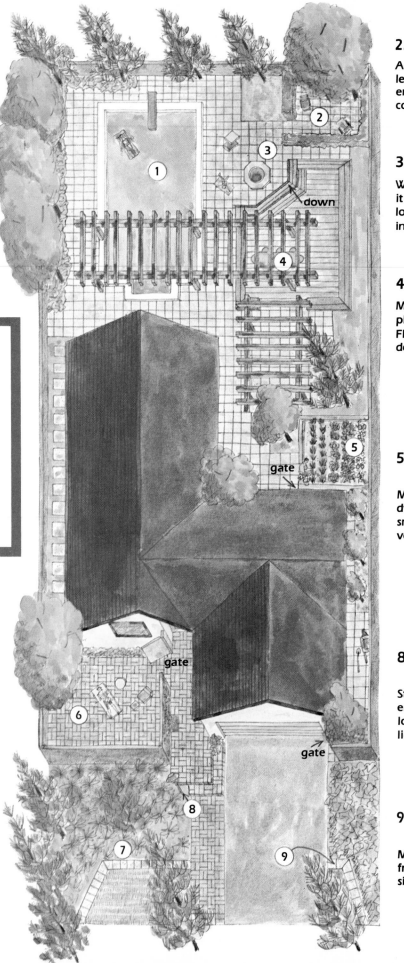

1. Recreation

Swimming pool is entered on broad steps — the grand way. Sweeping arbor overhangs water at one end.

Garden design

The well-thought-out plan at right satisfies nine landscaping goals, also offers these features: 1) Unconventional arbor extends over pool for hot climates; 2) Detached deck with built-in seating; 3) Gates close off entire rear yard and vegetable plot/utility area; 4) Several separate seating areas; 5) Minimum of lawn; 6) Privacy at front entrance.
Design: Roy Rydell.

6. Privacy

Walled patio by front door creates enclosure for relaxing, small parties.

7. Beautification

Trees and shrubs frame and screen house, soften neighborhood.

2. Comfort

Additional area for leisure: in shrub-enframed rear corner of yard.

3. Flexibility

When fire pit is not is use, it can be covered with low table for games, informal dining.

4. Entertaining

Meals and parties take place on deck under arbor. Floating candles sometime decorate pool at night.

5. Food Production

Mini-orchard of three dwarf fruit trees leads to small summer, winter vegetable garden

8. Safety and convenience

Steps leading to front entryway are lighted by low-voltage outdoor light.

9. Ease of maintenance

Mowing strips bordering front lawn sections simplify grass cutting.

The first step–select your goals

> *If you would be happy for a week, get married.*
> *If you would be happy for a month, kill your pig.*
> *But to be happy for a lifetime, plant a garden.*
> —Old Chinese Proverb

Landscaping makes a world of difference—and it tells the world a lot about you. The plants and structures that surround your home reflect your taste, your pleasures, your activities, your personality—*and* your planning.

Why tolerate a yard that isn't living up to its promise? Say it's uninspired: you don't get that special lift when you stride into your entryway. Or say it's lawn-heavy: you're oppressed by mowing chores every weekend.

Say it's inconvenient: no vine-draped terrace invites you to cool off and relax on a torrid summer day. Even say it's unfriendly, lacking eating and recreation areas that would encourage friends to gather in your garden. But don't despair. All of these minuses can be turned into pluses with some thoughtful landscaping.

Landscaping, of course, takes some doing. It calls for planning, money, work, and time. But it produces results. And not every expenditure of money, work, time, and thought gives such lasting satisfaction.

Making the outdoors livable

Contemporary landscaping ideas began to develop when homeowners decided they wanted to cook and entertain outdoors. Often they found, though, that their garden was not designed for outdoor living. There was no privacy; tables and chairs poked holes in the lawn; the sun was too hot, the wind too strong, the evenings too chilly.

Soon it became clear that, if much the same kind of living is to take place outdoors as indoors, the same problems have to be solved—furniture arrangement; pathways for circulation; a floor of some sort for tables and chairs; walls (or fences or hedges) for privacy; and climate control. Landscaping means arranging outdoor space not only for beauty but also for comfort. It may mean paving a patio, constructing a deck, devising a sun or wind screen, installing lights, or building a roof over a garden corner. Landscaping sums up all the things one does to make a garden more livable.

What this book offers

Whether your garden spreads out for more than an acre or is only a mini-plot, the landscaping procedures are the same:
• Selecting and combining plants
• Shaping and planting the land
• Adding compatible structural elements

The purpose of this book is to explain these design principles and illustrate them with colorful photographs and drawings. In the pages that follow, ideas from gardening professionals nationwide are collected to help you transform your outdoor living areas into pleasure retreats.

You'll be well on your way if you design or remodel your garden with specific goals in mind (see below), remembering that the basis for all landscape design is the needs of the people using the yard (see page 32). You'll benefit, too, from the information on climate control on pages 19–21. These guidelines will show you how to block hot summer sun but invite warm winter rays, and to deflect disagreeable winds but catch refreshing or cooling breezes.

Know what you want

Homeowners who add plants and structures to their yards will usually achieve more successful results if they first identify their goals (see color photographs, pages 6–7). Foremost in their thoughts may be **beautification** of the property—highlighting attractive areas or drawing attention away from less inviting details. Another important aim is **privacy**, the desire for seclusion in a graceful setting away from the workaday world. A third goal can be to arrange for **comfort**, allowing you to stretch out to read on a shady patio or sip afternoon tea under a leafy arbor.

Of course, **safety and convenience** are vital factors in landscape planning. Does your traffic pattern lead visitors clearly to the front door, or do they sometimes knock at the kitchen door in confusion? Are paths and steps lighted? **Flexibility** is another quality homeowners must take into account. They may opt for a double-purpose bench whose seat opens for garden storage or a sandbox that can be covered to form a low dining table or a surface for container display. And then there's **recreation**—the croquet green, badminton court, horseshoe pits, or children's play yard that enhances a home environment.

Food production, a very practical goal, is becoming increasingly popular with homeowners who are partial to small vegetable gardens and fruit or nut trees. To others, outdoor **entertaining** is a recurrent pleasure; they may want to use their garden as a setting for a dinner party or barbecue or even as the site for a family wedding.

Finally, **ease of maintenance** is many a gardener's dream. Gardeners appreciate the benefits of such labor-saving ideas as mulching, mowing strips, raised planting beds, watering systems, and slow-growing plants. They plant easy-care trees (Grecian Laurel, loquat, Russian olive), shrubs (mahonia, ilex, forsythia), vines (clematis, trumpet vine, wisteria), and ground covers (sedum, liriope, cotoneaster).

Take time to identify your goals before you start a landscape plan. That way you'll more surely end up with the garden you want after the last spadeful of earth has been turned.

What professionals look for

Equipped with a background in both horticulture and design, landscape architects level a skillful eye on ragged homesites –both new and old –with an instinctive feeling for the elements needed to solve the landscape puzzle.

Landscape architects often help initially by asking them a few key questions. Then the professionals proceed to analyze the yard on the basis of four landscaping guidelines.

The three questions professionals ask

When you consult a landscape architect, you might expect to be asked these questions:

1) How does your family live? A family's life style should be the basis for designing a landscape plan. If sports are a popular activity, this consideration will help you decide how to allot space. If the family includes small children or dogs, sturdy plants may have to be chosen. Perhaps entertaining is important to the family; if so, this fact will influence the architect's plan. Or if a family is particularly fond of cultivating native plants, still another approach may be required.

2) If you're concerned with upgrading one problem area of your yard, how will doing this affect the whole garden? Suppose you're intent on adding a patio. Will doing this cut down on the amount of lawn area you will want? Or perhaps you want to plant a row of trees to add privacy to your front yard. Might this reduce the amount of sun you enjoy? Could you be creating unexpected problems — invasive tree roots, for example, or unusable planting space under the trees when they mature?

Professionals normally consider the garden as a whole. Even when landscaping or remodeling only a part of your yard, think of it in relation to the rest of your property, both for the present and for the future.

3) Do you understand materials and their uses? Make it your business to learn what can and cannot be done with wood, concrete, brick, plastics, and other materials. Study materials to understand their advantages and disadvantages; choose them accordingly. Concrete, for example, is a relatively inexpensive, strong, and versatile material that can be poured in many shapes. But unless it is specially finished with exposed aggregate or a color, a concrete surface may have a cold look. It can also crack easily on shifting land. And concrete walks and patios are a frequent cause of children's skinned knees.

The four basic landscaping guidelines

As they survey yards and plan for development or restoration, landscape architects tend to think in terms of four guiding principles: unity, balance, proportion, and variety.

Unity. An indiscriminate array of unrelated plants and structures results in a chaotic overall picture, much like a child's room at its messiest. Unifying the various landscaping materials is an essential part of creating a pleasurable garden.

A sense that everything belongs together may be achieved by repeating common garden elements. Grouping junipers at the patio edge, for example, and then repeating junipers in a line down a path, followed by another group at the path's end, ties one area of the garden in with another. Or you might choose white petu-

Knowing how big 1,000 square feet and 100 square feet are becomes important for the home gardener because most lawn and garden prescriptions are given for these size areas. Note that 1,000 square feet spans about 30 by 35 feet –or about half the size of a tennis court. And 100 square feet is 10 by 10 feet.

nias and dwarf yellow marigolds as a common border for bedding gardens throughout the yard.

Try to avoid planting too many distinctive areas that must be tied together. The more parts you break your garden into, the harder it will be to unify them.

Balance. A balanced distribution of landscaping elements produces a garden focal point. Balance (not symmetry) lies in creating the same visual weight on either side of a center of interest. A large tree to the left of the entryway, for example, may be balanced by two smaller trees, placed to the right; alone, the larger tree would draw the eye away from the focal point—the front door. The "weight" used to create balance need not be mass; instead, it can be color, form, or interest.

Proportion. Choose plants and garden structures that are in scale with the architectural lines of your home. An 80-foot poplar tree could easily overpower a diminutive one-story home. On the other hand, a single juniper 10 feet high would be lost at the corner of a two-story structure.

When selecting plants, always try to think ahead to the size of the mature plant. Though an 8-foot pine may fit nicely beside the house today, in a few years it could raise the roof.

Variety. Variety is related to surprise, a welcome element in any landscape scheme. The presence of a purple-leafed flowering plum in a predominantly green planting scheme is a welcome relief to the eye. So is the introduction of an exotic plant or two—a smoke tree or a *Ginkgo biloba*—amid more conventional plantings.

Even though variety can lessen the monotony that may result from striving for unity, many gardeners create stunning landscape effects with massed beds of a single variety or color of plant.

Add know-how to your plan

In working out your own design, you should be aware of the special devices used by leading landscape architects. Photographs of their work say over and over again:

• **Design generously,** then count costs.

To get a feeling of luxury in the garden (and where else can it be bought so cheaply?), you need only take a step beyond necessity here and there.

A brick walk, two-feet wide, laid in sand, can be changed to a luxurious 5-foot walk at a modest cost. A 10 by 16-foot patio seems more than adequate to most builders; but a 12 by 30-foot patio, part concrete, part ground cover, part gravel, is luxurious.

In most houses, the step between the house and the patio is only as wide as the door. Lengthen it and widen it, and you not only go in and out of the house with ease but you have a floor to support garden seats as well.

• **Design boldly** to prevent later plant growth from erasing your design.

Design should make a strong, definite statement. Unless you lead from strength, growing plants will erase the design almost as soon as it is executed. What may appear too strong the first year is softened and quieted by plant growth by the third year. The low wall, the wide mowing strip, the raised bed—these are strong, permanent lines.

If you live where water is a problem

In any region where scarcity of water is a concern, gardeners may have to shift their emphasis to plants that require little moisture.

Since a lawn uses more water per square foot than any other kind of ordinary landscaping, you may want to eliminate your lawn or reduce it to a small, cooling patch. Or you can replace lawn with unthirsty ground covers or low shrubs, crushed rock or gravel, river stones, bark and wood chips, brick on sand, or decking with space between the boards. All of these materials allow what rain there is to enter the soil rather than drain off.

Economy in watering may also be necessary. Hand watering is best done at windless times—night or early morning—to reduce evaporation. Drip irrigation—delivering water to individual plants through a system of narrow tubes or porous tubing—may be one of the most efficient methods ever devised for watering flowers, trees, shrubs, vines, crops. It can cut water use by 20 to 50 percent. A less expensive alternative is a soil soaker.

Mulching helps soil hold water by lessening evaporation. Cover root areas with such materials as lightly perforated black plastic film, composted manure or garden refuse, ground bark, leaves, old newspaper, sawdust, straw, or cultivated earth (a dust mulch).

Planting means watering. If your area is suffering from any kind of water shortage, postpone extensive planting until fall. This way, nature does (or should do) the watering for you. Even if rain is not forthcoming, what watering you do at this season will go farther.

Following are suggestions for plants that will survive with a minimum of water:

Annuals and perennials. See the list of drought-resistant annual and perennial plants on page 79.

Ground covers. Arctostaphylos uva-ursi, Cotoneaster (check your nurseryworker for best varieties), Euonymus fortunei radicans, Hypericum calycinum, Juniper (check your nurseryworker for best varieties), Rosmarinus officinalis 'Prostratus', Vinca minor.

Hedges, screens, and borders. Abelia grandiflora, Maple (check your nurseryworker for best varieties), Cotoneaster divaricatus, Cupressus glabra, Dodonaea viscosa, Elaeagnus angustifolia, Hakea laurina, H. suaveolens, Laurus nobilis, Ligustrum ovalifolium, Myrtus communis, Nerium oleander, Photinia fraseri, Pinus nigra, P. resinosa, Pyracantha coccinea, Santolina chamaecyparissus, Teucrium chamaedrys, Viburnum opulus 'Nanum', Xylosma congestum.

Plants to cascade over a wall. Arctostaphylos uva-ursi, Ceanothus griseus horizontalis, Cistus salvifolius, Cotoneaster adpressa, C. dammeri, C. horizontalis, Juniperus conferta, J. horizontalis 'Douglasii', Pelargonium peltatum, Rosmarinus officinalis 'Prostratus', Sollya fusiformis, Vinca minor.

Basic shrubs. Cotoneaster horizontalis, Juniper (check your nurseryworker for best varieties), Mahonia aquifolium, Pinus mugo mughus, Prunus ilicifolia, Rosmarinus officinalis.

Small and medium-size trees. Acer ginnala, Albizia julibrissin, Arbutus unedo, Betula verrucosa, Cercis canadensis, Cladrastis lutea, Crataegus lavallei, Elaeagnus angustifolia, Eriobotrya japonica, Ginkgo biloba, Gleditsia triacanthos inermis, Koelreuteria paniculata, Lagerstroemia indica, Malus, Nerium oleander, Olea europaea, Pistacia chinensis.

Vines. Ampelopsis brevipedunculata, Bougainvillea, Campsis radicans, Grape, Hedera helix, Hydrangea anomala petiolaris, Honeysuckle (check your nurseryworker for best varieties), Polygonum aubertii, Wisteria.

Follow five design principles

Most people recognize the difference between combinations of garden elements that are pleasing and those that are jarring to the eye. In well-landscaped gardens, the following principles of design are taken into account:

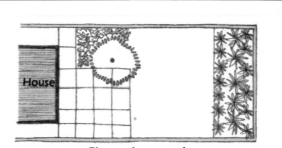

1. If the relation between things is either too nearly equal or extremely unequal, the sight of them is disturbing.

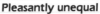

Pleasantly unequal

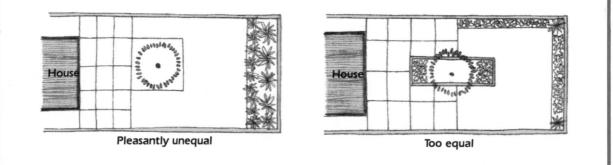

Pleasantly unequal

Too equal

2. When organizing space, remember that most people recognize orderliness in well-known shapes.

The simplest shapes the designer can work with are squares, rectangles, triangles, and circles.

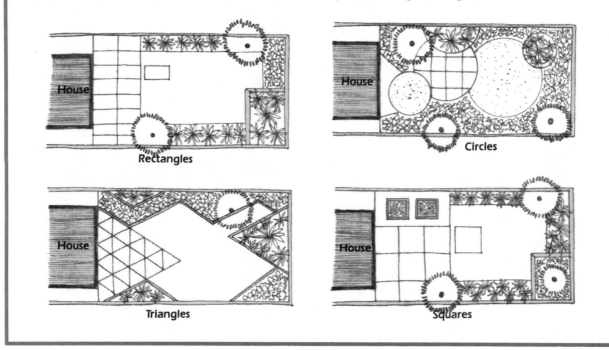

Rectangles

Circles

Triangles

Squares

3. Plantings and structures should be arranged to satisfy the need for seclusion. But to carry design so far that it prevents the home dweller from walking and playing in the garden will arouse a cooped-up feeling—the very feeling most people come into the garden to escape.

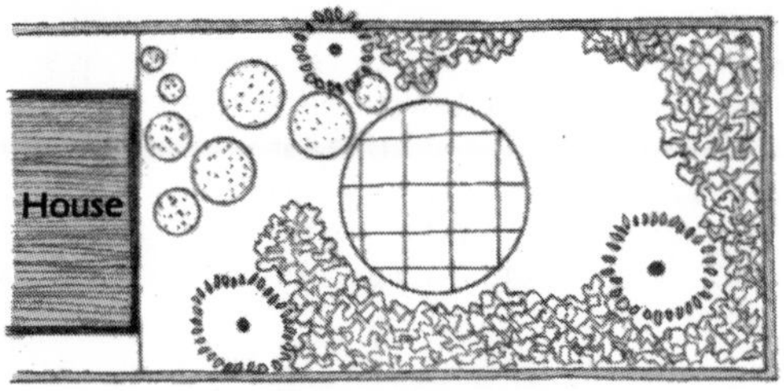

Adequate feeling of shelter

Overplanted

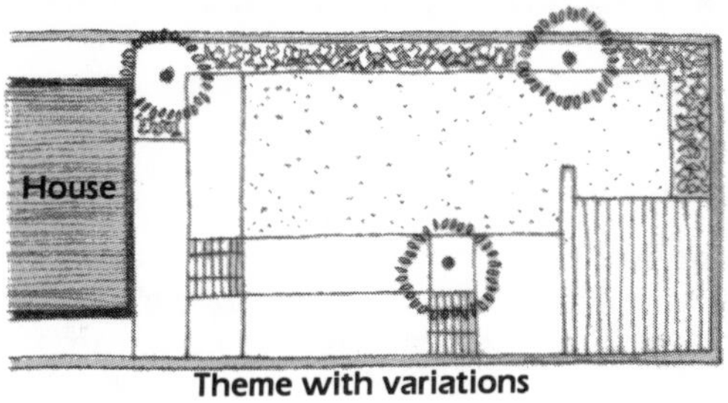

Theme with variations

Theme with variations

4. The eye is not disturbed by a change if an easily recognizable shape carries through the main theme. Such a theme with variations creates a unified garden, maximizing variety and interest and minimizing monotony. Above are two examples showing many variations—in paving, overhead, fence, lawn, and raised bed—of a basic theme.

5. In grouping shapes or masses, it is much easier to make them seem unified by joining or interlocking the units than by separating them and putting them in tension with one another.

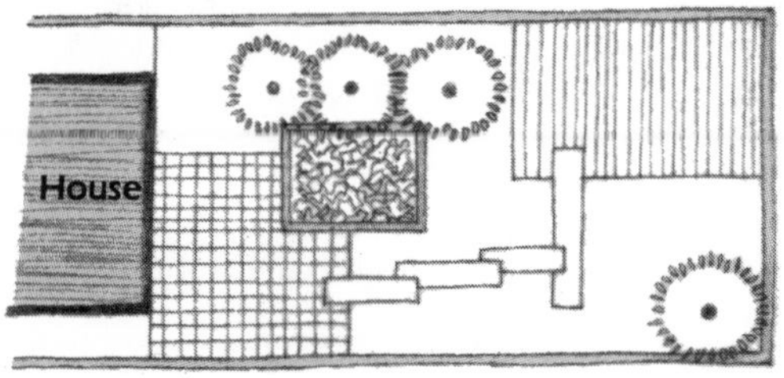

Interlocked

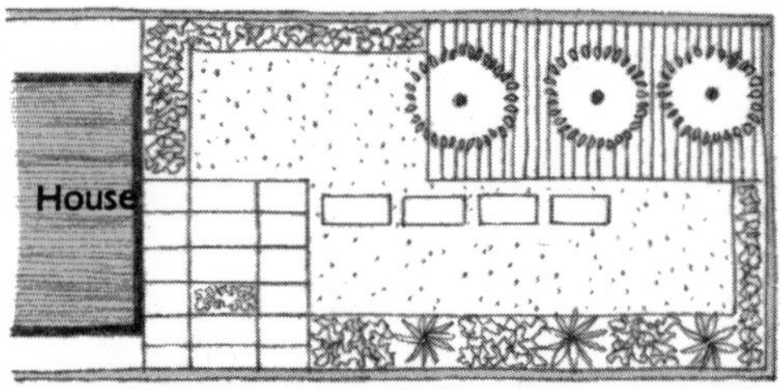

Tension; not unified

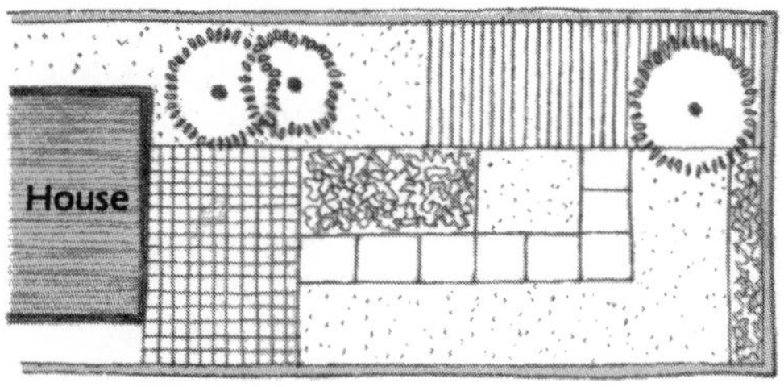

Joining

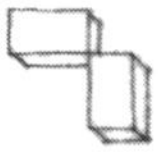

First a pencil, then a spading fork

The surest way to combine harmoniously the landscape elements you want is to sketch them out on paper before you begin to work. (An alternative way is to outline your patio, lawn, and planting areas on the ground with string attached to stakes. This approach allows you to check your plan by walking through it.)

Planning on paper

In putting your plan on paper, you'll save yourself hours of measuring if you can first locate any of the following:

1) Deed map. Shows actual dimensions and orientation of your property. If you do not have this, you might get information at the city hall, county courthouse, title company, bank, or mortgage company.

2) Contour map. For hill sites this is very important. It shows 1-foot, 2-foot, 5-foot, or 10-foot contours—the exact *shape* of your site. It may also indicate property dimensions, streets, sidewalks, utilities, large trees, rocks and other elements.

3) Architect's drawings or house plans. Should show site plan, floor plan, elevations, relation to site, windows, doors, roof, utilities, hose bib connections, downspouts, footing details.

Make a large map on graph paper (24 by 36 inches) that will show in clear detail just exactly what you have to work with. Draw to the largest scale the paper will allow—generally, ¼ inch equaling 1 foot. This will be your **base map.** Later, by slipping this base map under the top sheet on a pad of tracing paper, you can sketch out designs to your heart's content.

Show the following on your base map:

• Boundaries and dimensions of the lot.
• Orientation to the compass—indicate hot spots and shade areas.
• Direction of prevailing wind throughout the year.
• Location of easements that may affect your planning—underground telephone lines, trunk sewers (see your deed map).
• Location of setback boundaries that may limit outdoor building. Check with your local building official about restrictions on such things as height and placement of fences, detached and attached structures, and ordinances regulating swimming pools.
• Location and depth of utility connections—water, gas, and sewer; underground electric or telephone wires; outlets on outside of house for water and electricity; sewer cleanouts; septic tank drain field; meter boxes.
• Location of your house. Show all doors and windows and indicate from which room they open.
• Soil conditions—show location of fills, cuts. If you want, make test borings to determine character of soil (generally not necessary when remodeling an existing garden).

• Gradient—show contour lines; locate high and low points; indicate contours on neighboring property that will affect your planning by draining water into your garden; mark downspouts and indicate whether these lead to underground drains or sewer connections.
• Map existing plants, particularly large, established trees; indicate names of plants, if known.
• Alongside plot plan, note the problems beyond the lot line, such as good or bad views of neighbors' properties, hills, trees, telephone poles.

When you have gathered in front of you all the physical restrictions and requirements imposed by your lot, do some preliminary sketches on tracing paper laid over the base map. Experiment with the relationships of space and plane and of form and line until the design suits you. Using the circle as the basic theme, identify the separate areas you want—for example, lawn, storage, play, service, patio (see drawing 2 on facing page).

Asking the key questions

The next step is to define specifics. Locate the entrance area and decide how you want to handle it. Do you want your front yard open or private? Do you want this area to be lawn, patio, or ground cover?

For a patio, will you need an overhead, trees, or fencing for climate control? Where will you place the clothesline? Can garbage containers be handy but hidden? Should a growing area for cut flowers be included? Should the children's yard be surfaced in pavement, lawn, or bark? How should screening be used to visually separate various parts of the yard? Should the garden be enclosed? Would fencing, plantings, or a combination of the two be most effective? How should pathways be situated so traffic flows easily around the house and garden? All of these items are considered in drawings 3 and 4 on the facing page.

Now let's follow the steps in making a landscape sketch.

1) On a sheet of tracing paper laid over the base map, we indicate the living areas desired and their approximate location, showing where sun and wind protection will be needed. When we remove the tissue, it may look something like this.

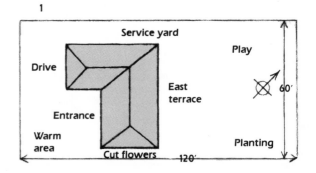

2) We then draw circles of various sizes to indicate the relative dimensions of various areas: lawn, storage, play yard, streetside terrace, and so on. At this time, based on the use of space and on sun and wind control, we might continue to adjust the relationship of elements until the design suits us.

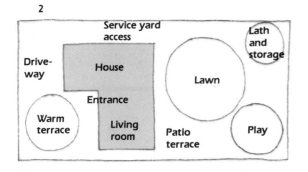

3) Next, let's take care of the entrance areas, patio, and paved surfaces. Since we wish the patio to be an extension of the living room, its location is fixed. Dotted lines indicate the patio area we intend to cover with a rectangular overhead. Though we have a placed a partial circle of trees around the lawn, we may later decide to fill out this circle in order to screen off the lath and storage area.

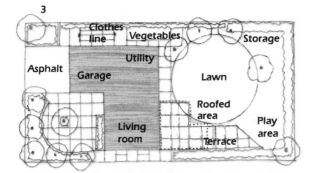

Now let's get traffic under control by providing paved areas from the driveway to the entrance, around the house, and in the garden.

4) With the exception of trees, all planting up to this point has been on the ground. The trick now is to place plants and structures in the vertical plane. At this point, think in tems of height and width rather than considering specific plants or structures.

As we develop the plan, we will indicate each step by a letter (see below):

A. Entrance court (south side of house) is partially screened from street by shrub and tree planting. Will be used as outdoor sitting room when sun is wanted.

B. Clotheslines are screened from street view by front fence panel.

C. Since circle of trees planted to slow down wind from the northwest won't amount to much the first 2 years, a circular screen fence 6 feet high is built.

D. Area behind fence will be used for cutting garden, garden work center, or both.

E. Area for children's play yard equipment. Actually, children have choice of lawn for games or paved area completely around the house for wheeled toys.

F. Lawn panel.

G. Paved terrace in 5 by 5-foot squares with 2 by 4-inch headers between squares.

H. Lath overhead protects from hot midsummer afternoon sun on north side of house.

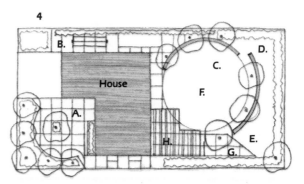

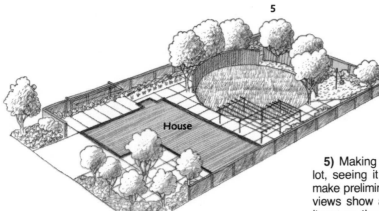

5) Making plan views—looking straight down at your lot, seeing it in two dimensions—is the easiest way to make preliminary arrangements of space and volume. Plan views show at a glance the relationships among all the items on the lot. However, you should also try to think in perspective—in three dimensions—as you plan on paper.

If we visualized the garden as it would appear from a nearby hill, we would see it in perspective. It would look like what you see in this drawing—a balanced landscape design that has grown from step-by-step planning.

Modules make everything fit

When planning landscape designs on paper, many people find it helpful to work with a single unit of space –a square or rectangle –repeated over and over again, like squares on a checkerboard or bricks in a wall. Working with a uniform module helps you to put more exactness in step-by-step preliminary planning.

How to work with modules

Your module might be 3 by 4 feet, 4 by 4, 4 by 5, or almost any larger rectangle that suits your needs. Using a rectangular module makes everything fall neatly into place; there's no question about what spacings to use or what sizes to establish.

If you decide to use a 4 by 5-foot module, all of your walks would be 4 feet or a generous 5 feet in width. Your patio would divide up into 4 by 5 rectangles. One or more of these might be an open 4 by 5-foot planting island within your patio area. Plant beds would be 4 feet across. A sandbox might be 8 by 10 feet, a raised bed 4 by 5 or 4 by 10 feet, a tree well 4 by 5 or 8 by 10 feet.

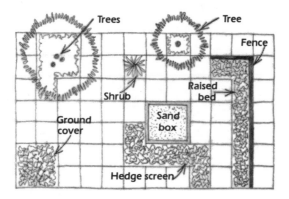

Besides giving a sense of order to your garden scheme, the module system offers other advantages. With the suggested dimensions, you have only 12, 16, or 20 square feet of paving to worry about at any one time. You can mix and pour concrete for just one rectangle at a time. You can lay one rectangle of bricks before you start another. If you're a little bit off with your brick courses, you can get a fresh start with the next rectangle.

Selecting your module. The length of the house wall adjoining the proposed patio can help you determine what size module to use. If the wall is 24 feet long, for instance, a 4-foot division in your patio paving would make 6 modules fit your wall dimension exactly. If you plan to work with bricks, avoid brick cutting by making your module an exact multiple of brick dimensions. Most professionals urge a module no less than 3 by 3 feet; amateur landscapers say a generous module saves work.

Designing the modular way. Using the base map described on page 14, here's how to work out a design using the modular system:

A. Using a 5-foot-square unit, the entire lot was ruled off in 5-foot squares. The length of the house divides by 5, and the walks at the side of the house will be 5 feet wide.

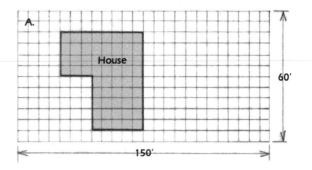

B. For a paved area out from the living room, three squares were marked out, giving a generous width of 15 feet. For length, 6 panels of 30 feet were allowed, providing extra space for plantings. (See sketch below.)

C. An overhead lath was included to protect a section of the patio from the sun and the wind. For added protection from the north wind, the north end was closed off with a fence.

D. A raised bed with a seat wall was included, bordering the lawn area. A wood screen was added behind the raised bed for privacy. Room was left beyond the screen for a children's area or a service area.

E. To get away from the rectangular feeling that this design was creating, trees for shade and wind protection were planted in a circular pattern.

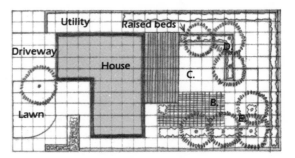

The facing page shows four other ways to design this same rectangular lot. In each example, space has not been designated for service, storage, or play. According to your habits, interests, and needs, you can locate these areas alongside the house or take some room away from the planted area. Each design involves a 5 by 5-foot module.

Four more ways to landscape a rectangular lot

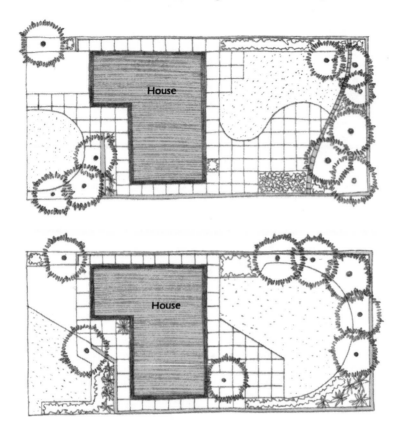

Free-flowing design

The U-shaped front lawn and trio of trees, curving back lawn, terrace, and planted trees all contribute to a graceful, unified sweeping line. The large patio supplies ample outdoor living space.

Spacious lawn

A generous grassy area is ringed by a privacy screen and simple planting of trees. The angle of the back patio and lawn occurs again in front with lawn and planting bed slanting off the driveway.

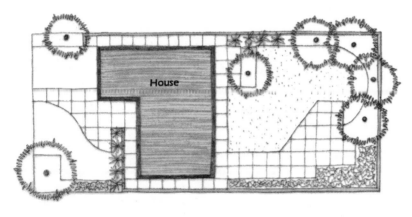

Various geometric shapes

Variety highlights this design. The back patio juts into a section of lawn, as does a planting bed. Planted trees complement the lawn's curve. In front, the free-flowing lawn borders an L-shaped planting bed.

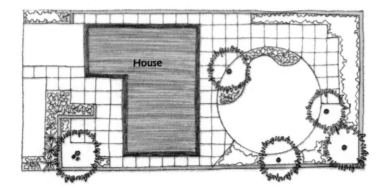

Circular lawn

A large grassy circle softens rectangular home and lot shapes. A curved planting bed partially separates patio and lawn. Perimeter plantings give privacy, serve as a backdrop to the patio, lawn. Front area combines entry court, plants, small lawn.

Garden style – the choices are many

A British-born couple, consulting a landscape designer in Tucson, told him, "Basically, we're 17th century people. Give us a 17th century garden." And he did.

Perhaps your taste does not run toward a formal, European-style garden. Still, landscape planning works better if you have some unifying idea of the style you prefer.

What are the possibilities? Here are eight different types of gardens to consider. In making a choice, keep in mind this principle: select a garden style that is compatible with your home's style.

FORMAL. Among the plants most commonly found in a formal garden are boxwood and privet hedges, topiary forms (of eugenia, boxwood, myrtle, or privet), a rose garden, and an herb garden. Trees and shrubs are normally placed in orderly rows. Structural elements often include a sundial, statuary and other traditional garden art, and a central fountain. (See the formal garden pictured on page 49.)

CONTEMPORARY. Garden elements in "now" landscapes include such medium-size trees as silk tree, hawthorn, and birch; flowering shrubs — India hawthorn, citrus, heather — grouped seminaturally; and flowering ground covers — gazania, carpet bugle, ice plant, and mondo grass. Contemporary gardens sometimes feature decks, small pools, spas, and evening lighting. (See the contemporary garden pictured on page 32.)

DRY GARDEN. Landscaping to create a dry garden can generate high drama with such plantings as ocotillo, yuccas, agaves, tamarisks, Jerusalem thorn, small palms, fan palms, cactus, and succulents. (For other unthirsty plants, see page 11.) Representative structural touches: boulders, exposed aggregate concrete walks, adobe walls, native rock walls, and an artificial wash of sand and gravel. (See the drought-resistant garden pictured on page 49.)

SHADE. Gardens having generous shady areas are naturals for such shade-loving plants as camellias, azaleas, rhododendrons, begonias, ferns, ivies, and aucuba. If you want to *provide* shade, plant these trees: ash, ginkgo, honey locust, maple, oak, or tulip tree. Structures that will be pleasantly shady summer retreats include patio overheads, arbors, lath houses, and gazebos. (See the shade garden pictured on page 6.)

TROPICAL. If you want plants that give a tropical appearance but do not require a tropical climate, choose from among these: acanthus, angelica tree, wild ginger, aucuba, bergenia, canna, catalpa, loquat, Japanese aralia, ferns, hosta, mahonia, empress tree, castor bean, calla lily, lily-of-the-Nile, cordyline, iris, New Zealand flax, and yucca. Favorite structural elements are lanais, footbridges, and displays of running water, particularly waterfalls.

RUSTIC. Naturalized plantings of spring bulbs fit well into the rustic scene. So do oaks, pines, and large-leafed deciduous trees such as sugar maple, tulip tree, or London plane tree. Plants that provide autumn color — liquidambar, sour gum, larch, ginkgo, sorrel tree — also adapt very well, as do plants with colorful berries, such as dogwood, cotoneaster, pyracantha, barberry, skimmia, and holly. Such structural elements as rough-hewn fences, randomly placed boulders, and elements giving the impression of water (a gravel stream bed, for instance) complete the picture. (See the garden pictured on page 28.)

ORIENTAL. Here typical plantings include bamboo, dwarf conifer, Japanese maple, azalea, flowering cherry, and other flowering fruit trees. Complementary structures might be tea houses, stone lanterns, bamboo fences, and water basins with bamboo flumes. Areas of raked sand or garden beds of stones also figure importantly.

NATIVE PLANTS. A drive through nearby countryside to see what's growing in the wild will be your best guide here. Or ask your local nurseryworker to identify natives that thrive best in gardens in your region. Randomly placed boulders and steps or fences built of split or whole logs are effective structural touches in a garden of native plants. (See the native plant garden pictured on page 49.)

Your decision about a garden style will determine many things: the kind of plants you buy; the type of structures you add; and the design of fences, gates, and walks. The style you choose, of course, should be compatible with your family's life style. Once you've settled on the garden's appearance, you'll find that a unified style will lend a touch of distinction to your property, both enhancing its livability and adding considerably to its value. And sometimes — as in the case of an oriental garden — borrowing a garden style from another country will give you fresh insights into another culture.

Controlling the climate

In planning how you want your garden to look, it's important to consider a yard's existing conditions. One of the most significant factors to weigh is the climate –the sun's path and the wind's direction.

Here comes the sun

The path of the sun and its intensity through the hours of the day and the seasons of the year affect the location and type of outdoor living area you plan and determine the kind of plants you grow.

If the number of warm, sunny days is limited, you naturally wish to develop areas where the sun can be trapped. You appreciate paved areas of concrete and brick that absorb the sun's heat and reradiate it to increase the temperature near their surfaces. Where the amount of sun is limited, look to south walls to reflect extra heat for those plants that need it; avoid plantings that will shut off the sun in fall, winter, and spring.

If summer temperatures are high, you will want to temper the sun with overhead structures or screens of foliage and to minimize the amount of unshaded paving.

In western North America, the sun is never directly overhead. This means that a tree or overhead structure will

Sun and shade on a west-facing patio

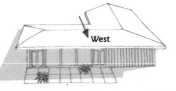

December 21, 11 A.M. *Patio is almost completely in shade. For morning sunshine, the usual solution is to continue patio around corner on south side.*

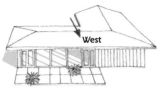

December 21, 4 P.M. *Late western sun sweeps across patio, flooding living room. If low-angled sun is uncomfortable, block with screen of tall shrubs, small trees.*

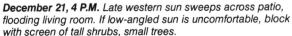

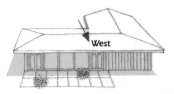

June 21, 11 A.M. *Throughout the year, the west side of the house has morning shade and afternoon sun. If you grow plants on this side, be sure they tolerate heat extremes.*

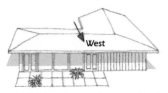

June 21, 4 P.M. *Try to intercept sun's rays with vines, trees, or structures to avoid west wall's heat input that reradiates into rooms of house after sundown.*

Sun and shade on a south-facing patio

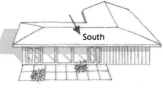

December 21, 11 A.M. *Sun's arc is at lowest point: rays flood across south patio from mid-morning to sundown. If patio is protected from wind, December sun will feel warmer.*

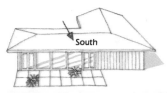

December 21, 4 P.M. *In cold-winter areas, low winter sun provides warmth on south-facing patio and rooms. In mild-winter areas, you may need some screening.*

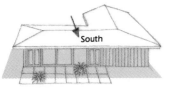

June 21, 11 A.M. *South patio is at its best when sun is high overhead. This orientation is good where summers are short and extra warmth is welcome in spring and fall.*

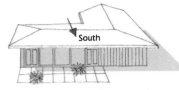

June 21, 4 P.M. *Late afternoon shade pattern leaves much of patio area in sun. There will be less shade from this day on. Block sun by plantings at patio's west side.*

never cast all of its shade directly beneath itself.

See the illustrations on page 19 for sun and shade patterns on a west patio and a south patio. Either a south or west orientation is perhaps the best location in the temperate climate zone because the sun provides warmth during the afternoon and early evening when you are most likely to use your patio. A north-facing patio will almost always be in the shade; this might be ideal if you live in an extremely warm climate zone. An east-oriented patio will receive morning sun and afternoon shade. This situation is less desirable if you want to use the patio in the evening. However, such an orientation might be perfect if you live in a warm climate or enjoy breakfast or brunch on the patio.

Study the wind

Make a careful study of the wind pattern around your house and over your lot. Too much wind blowing across an outdoor sitting area on a cool day can be as unpleasant as no breeze at all on a hot summer day. The idea is to control the wind—block it by fences, screens, or plants, or modify its flow to suit your needs.

To determine your prevailing winds, notice the "lean" of the trees in your neighborhood. The direction of the prevailing wind around your house may not be the same as around the house next door, however. Wind flows like water—spilling over obstacles, breaking into several currents, eddying and twisting.

It is unlikely that anyone experiences exactly the same temperature as the thermometer at the weather bureau. When the weather bureau says that the temperature is 68°, it means that a thermometer in the shade, protected from the wind, reads 68°. If there is a 10 to 15-mile-an-hour breeze, a person in the shade in the breeze may feel that the temperature is about 62°. If the breeze is stopped and the patio is in sunlight, the person will feel a comfortable 75° to 78°.

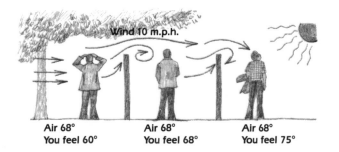

Air 68°
You feel 60°

Air 68°
You feel 68°

Air 68°
You feel 75°

In checking the wind problem around your house, remember that the house itself is your biggest windbreak. However, it may need additions to be effective. In some cases, the wind spills over the house and drops on the patio.

Following are the results of a *Sunset* study in wind control. (Lower line of figures shows number of feet from fence; upper line notes sensible temperature differences between these points and fence's windward side.)

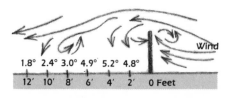

Wind washes over solid fence as stream of water would wash over a solid barrier. At about the distance equal to fence height, protection drops rapidly. Twelve feet away, you feel 1.8° warmer than in unprotected area.

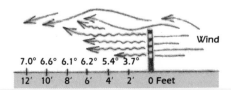

For fence with laths spaced about ½ inch apart, the lowest reading is close to the fence; the highest, 12 feet away. At 12 feet you would feel 7° warmer than when standing on windward side of the fence.

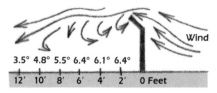

A 45° baffle at top of fence eliminates the downward crash of wind. In this pocket, and 6 feet away from fence, you feel 6.4° warmer than without a barrier. Beyond this point, temperature difference declines gradually.

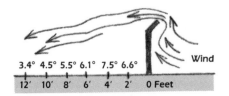

Angling baffle into wind gives greatest protection close to fence of any control tested. Beyond the maximum 7.5° increase, the comfort drop is gradual; effective protection extends to a distance more than twice fence height.

Take the seasons into account

The opportunities for outdoor living are greater in mild climates than in severe climates. However, completely comfortable outdoor living, hour after hour and day after day, is very rare. But each step you take to modify the climate increases the number of days you can use the outdoors.

If you pave an area immediately adjacent to the house, that area can be used between rain showers when the lawn would be too wet. If you control the breeze that sweeps across the patio, you can enjoy the patio in sunlight when air temperatures are much lower than the accepted 78° comfort temperature. A solid glass or plastic overhead allows patio use on rainy days.

Climate control—a classic example

The problem:

One of the best ways to understand how landscaping can modify climate for a house and yard is to start from scratch, as in this first drawing. Unchecked exposure to sun and wind causes uncomfortable living conditions.

Western sun hits glass, heating room

West wind sweeps across rear yard

Living room feels small, boxlike

Awkward, restrictive 2-foot level change from living room to ground

Outdoor area in full view of neighbor

The solution:

Here's how to create a livable, pleasant environment both indoors and out. Besides controlling the climate, the design offers the further benefits of adding beauty to the site and increasing the amount of available living space.

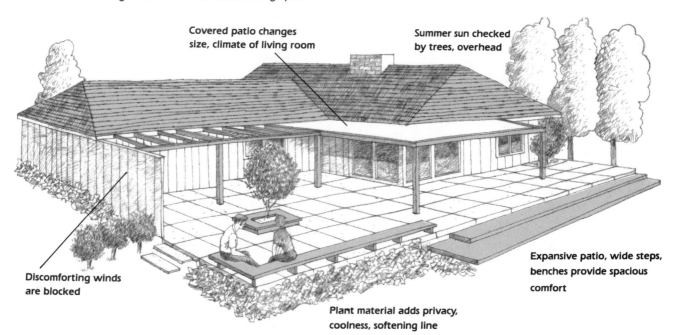

Covered patio changes size, climate of living room

Summer sun checked by trees, overhead

Discomforting winds are blocked

Expansive patio, wide steps, benches provide spacious comfort

Plant material adds privacy, coolness, softening line

The way to garden success

If you study a successful landscaping job to discover what makes it work so well, you'll probably find that the designer has used one or more of the esthetic guidelines described here and on page 25. As you plan for your new or remodeled garden, observe these five points – they can open the way to distinctive grounds. Garden designs: Roy Rydell.

Try for different levels

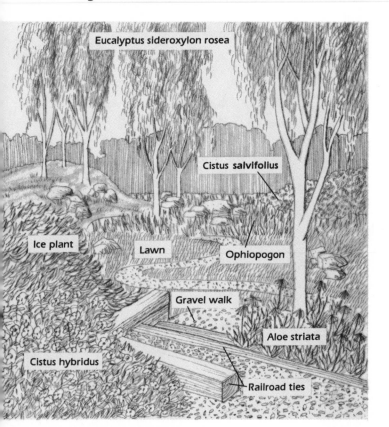

Eucalyptus sideroxylon rosea
Cistus salvifolius
Ice plant
Lawn
Ophiopogon
Gravel walk
Aloe striata
Cistus hybridus
Railroad ties

Grade change is an important—and often overlooked—feature of landscaping. By sculpturing the land to form berms and swales (berms are small mounds of soil; swales are depressions in the land), a gardener can stimulate visual interest and provide the illusion of expanded space. As a practical effect of grade change, rainfall can be drained off through shallow indentations at the same time that the adjacent mounded soil creates an improved plant nurturing environment.

If emphasized by steps and planting beds, even a drop of only 8 inches from a terrace to a lower level can add special interest to a piece of property. (For examples, see page 35.)

Use outdoors to extend indoors

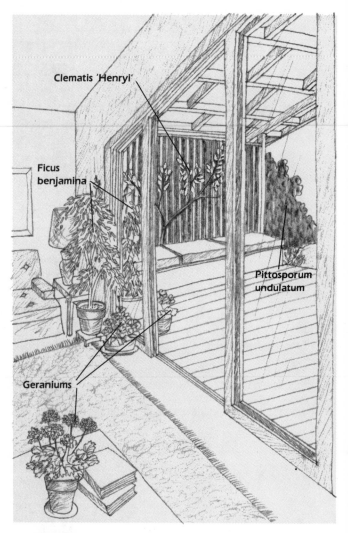

Clematis 'Henryi'
Ficus benjamina
Pittosporum undulatum
Geraniums

You enlarge a room visually when you develop the space beyond its windows to coordinate with the room's elements. In the drawing, you see that the living room has been extended visually on three planes. The deck acts as a visual extension of the interior floor. The wind screen, with its cushioned bench, reflects the interior wall. Also relating exterior space to the interior ceiling is the rather open patio roof, which inhibits wind flow but lets ample sunshine through.

Using similar plants on both sides of the window further emphasizes the relationship by bringing some of the garden inside the room. Try coordinating plant color, texture, and shape for subtle effects. And you should choose outdoor furniture that complements the style of indoor pieces.

Hawthorn trees

Rhododendrons

Trumpet vine

Marguerite daisies

Agapanthus

Lawn

Violets

Geraniums

Ivy

Plant for emphasis

A striking point of emphasis in the yard illustrated is the grouping of formally clipped trees; in a more informal garden, the same principle could be followed, giving nature a freer hand. Here, two areas of the garden are separated by a growing element that divides but does not conceal. Instead, the parallel tree trunks, equidistant from each other, and the mass of elevated foliage frame a series of views.

A less obvious but powerful effect in this garden is the tree foliage's strong shadow, which slowly shifts across the ground throughout the day. Sunlight can be an important ally in landscape design. In planting, place some elements so they will be spotlighted by the sun against shadowed backgrounds. Place other elements in the shade so they will be silhouetted against a clear, sunny sky or against a wall, basking in reflected light. The sun's course offers a dynamic element; take advantage of it.

Conceal, don't reveal all at once

The large tree in the foreground of this pictured garden has a double purpose: it makes the background scene recede and it conceals a bit of what lies beyond. In addition to the tree, some shrubs, flower beds, fences, hedges, and other trees are arranged to screen portions of the garden from initial view. This principle of gradual revelation of a landscape scene is frequently used in Japanese gardens. The series of slight surprises gradually meeting the eye as one moves through the garden is a mark of sophisticated design.

Southern magnolia

Malus arnoldiana

Raphiolepis

Ajuga

Portuguese laurel

Hydrangea

Six combinations of plants

Cordyline stricta, Fatsia japonica, Soleirolia (left to right). Though these shade-loving plants all have somewhat glossy leaves, the character of their leaves varies considerably.

Magnolia grandiflora, Pittosporum tobira 'Variegata', *Trachelospermum jasminoides* (left to right). Magnolia and star jasmine both have shiny leaves and white blossoms; pitttosporum has leaves of a grayer green and off-white with a duller texture.

Viburnum davidii, Acer palmatum, Pachysandra terminalis, (left to right). Viburnum has a large leaf with a distinctive crinkle. As a ground cover, pachysandra sprouts glossy leaves that have a complicated shape. In contrast, the maple's leaves are small in scale—like the tree itself—and deciduous.

Enkianthus, Kurume azalea, Maidenhair fern (left to right). Enkianthus offers a striking silhouette and fall coloring; azalea texture is very even and small-scaled; the five-finger fern has a delicate but strong pattern.

Tibouchina semidecandra, Agapanthus africanus, Echeveria elegans (left to right). With its straplike leaves, agapanthus provides a strong contrast to tibouchina, a lush, flamboyant, brilliantly blooming small tree with velvety leaves. Though the leaves of echeveria also have a velvety texture, they are gray in color.

Acacia baileyana, Euryops, Cotoneaster microphylla (left to right). Producing fernlike gray foliage, acacia features cascades of yellow pompon flowers. Also gray and bearing yellow flowers, euryops has contrasting, coarsely indented leaves. Cotoneaster displays fine-textured, dull leaves and berries.

Vary color, texture, and shape

Plants can sometimes offer gardeners the perplexing challenge of displaying them so they will show off to best advantage. One of the easiest ways to do this is to place a plant beside another that is quite unlike it in color, texture, or shape. You've seen this done in simple ways—the striking combination of fiery red and snowy white petunias, for example. But greater variety and subtlety of contrastive effects is also possible—and often desirable.

• **Color.** A single massed color makes a bold, commanding statement that is just as effective from a distance as it is close up. Colors that are mixed for interesting variety, though, are best placed so they can be appreciated close at hand. From a distance, colors dilute one another, and variety loses its force.

Sometimes a single plant can offer a pleasing range of colors. Indoors, coleus is a spectacular variegated example. Outdoor possibilities include multicolored flowers (sweet pea), ground covers (variegated ivy), and trees (variegated box elder). One especially interesting shrub —yesterday-today-and-tomorrow (*Brunfelsia calycina floribunda*)—flowers simultaneously in three shades of blue: light, medium, and dark. Whether color is diversified over a large planting bed or varied in a special plant, it provides a garden focal point.

• **Texture.** A leaf's surface can be as slick as glass or as rough as oak bark. By placing a bold, shiny plant such as English Laurel *(Prunus laurocerasus)* beside the spine-toothed, almost fernlike mahonia, you better accentuate the unique quality of each.

• **Shape.** Shape is the mass form of an individual element, or the total form created by the massing of similar elements. Sometimes you may create a unified planting by combining similar elements—for example, the grass-like shapes of mondo grass, lily-of-the-Nile, and *Liriope gigantea.* At other times you will want to try for great contrast. The possibilities are endless. Giving careful thought to plantings of varying shape, color, and texture will pay landscaping dividends.

On the facing page you will find illustrations of six possible groupings of plants that take advantage of contrasting color, texture, and shape. With this as a starting point, perhaps you can find inspiration to mix and match your own plants for the most striking effects.

Attracting admiration *is the 'Gartenmeister Bonstedt' fuchsia blooming in this garden. Robust star jasmine vine contrasts at right.*

How to make space work for you

One of the secrets of landscaping is knowing how to change a liability into an asset. This is especially useful in designing for a lot that is smaller than one might expect or that is shaped in a seemingly unpromising way. Even in the most awkward situation, artful landscaping can do wonders. It can create outdoor areas that, besides being functional, offer strong visual appeal, a sense of increased space, and pleasing elements of surprise.

Study these approaches to making the best use of space on four typically shaped lots. (The arrows on the drawings indicate the direction in which a viewer's attention is drawn by the landscape elements.) Landscape designs: Roy Rydell.

Square lot

If a lot is square, the roughly rectangular space often remaining for outside use can be pleasantly modified by group plantings and structures with contrasting configurations. In the drawing, an oval-shaped lawn artfully varies the angular lines of the lot and house. For variety, two areas of interest are faced off at either end of the rear garden. Leaving the house, one may look left toward a circle of "trees" with high-pruned trunks. (Actually these are deciduous shrubs of vertical growth habit, planted closely enough together to encourage them to reach up for light.) Within this circle is a concealed glade—a mecca for those seeking privacy. At the opposite end of the garden, facing the sun, is a small greenhouse. Other parts of the lot provide for a welcoming front entryway and space for essential activities.

Pie-shaped lot

Though this lot offers the advantages of minimum public space in front and maximum private space at the sides and in back, it presents the problem of how best to use the generous but irregularly shaped space. Here is one solution. Much of the area at the lot's front is paved to provide off-street parking for three cars. Off the cul-de-sac in front, a small group of plantings, screened from the rear gardens, creates a pleasant entryway. Deeper into the lot, three separate areas have been established around the living room wing, which projects into the main garden. Two of the areas have circular lawns ringed by trees; the lawns are proportionate in size to the spaces in which they are planted. To create a special mood for the central area, a semicircular paved area off the living room leads to a fanciful gazebo. In the back corner nearest to the house is space for a small vegetable garden; play space is provided in the far corner of the lot.

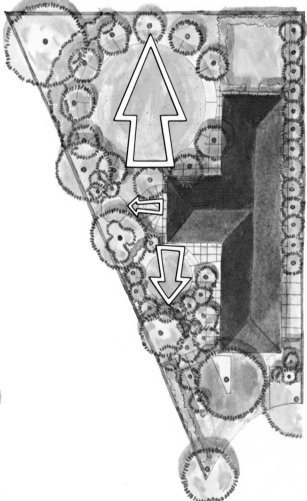

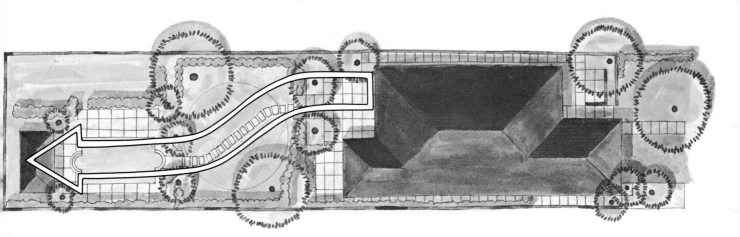

Long, narrow lot

To minimize the barber-pole effect of this type of lot, divide the space into two distinct areas that are offset, as shown in the drawing. Closest to the rear terrace of the house is a circular expanse of lawn, framed by a partial square of trees backed against the lot lines. The eye follows the S-curved axis along the stepping-stone path from the first garden to a somewhat separated second garden. Here you find the irresistible sparkle of a swimming pool along with its covered poolside shelter. A fairly large vegetable plot fits into the far corner of this area. Other gardens on the lot include a small terrace, screened from the work area by high shrubs and offering a private retreat off the master bedroom, and a walled courtyard providing usable outdoor living space by the entryway.

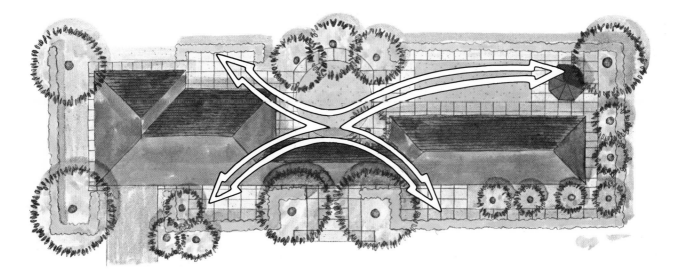

Extremely shallow lot

To use this kind of lot to best advantage, manipulate space visually by placing the outdoor living areas at the far ends of the lot. Because setback limitations eat up more open space on a shallow lot than on others, reclaiming some of that space for semiprivate use becomes a high priority. In this plan the entryway is expansive and welcoming. Low walls, hedges, and small trees surrounding small paved terraces beside the front entrance return a certain amount of public space to family use. An atrium-like court opposite the main entrance serves as a green core for the entire garden because of its small, tree-ringed, circular lawn. From here, one sees a gazebo at far right and an arbor-covered, built-in bench at left. Fruits and vegetables are grown near the utility area at far left.

Entryways:
first impressions matter

Graceful wrought iron gate leads through arched brick entryway to entrance off enclosed garden. Design: Robert E. Marvin.

Understated staggered-fence entryway, largely evergreen garden perfectly suit the mood of this home. Bold numbers make house easy to locate. Design: John Herbst, Jr.

Three-level brick entry court *accents the horizontal. Railroad-tie headers repeat theme of home's half-timbered walls. Foreground plants: left, juniper; right, liriope. Design: Galper/Baldon.*

Massive brick planters *delineate steps rising from sidewalk, driveway to front door. Design: Robert W. Chittock.*

Peek past *green gate to see color spectacular of petunias, geraniums. Design: Patrick Maas/William Benner.*

Hexagonal-tiled driveway and generous parking area, bordered by curving planting bed, adjoins shade garden and steps leading to pool.

2. Combining your

Shade garden *under spreading* Metrosideros excelsa *(New Zealand Christmas tree) blends handsomely with wide cantilevered steps abutting small boulders on each side. Design: Lang and Wood.*

plants with structures

Plan gardens with people in mind

Even a postage-stamp-size garden can live big, with table and chairs for outdoor meals (see cover), room for a lively game of croquet. Containers add splashy color. Design: R. David Adams.

The first concern in landscaping should be people. An effective measure of good landscape design is whether the planning allows people to satisfy their varying outdoor interests with no sacrifice of comfort. Here are some examples:

• Human height is the scale against which the sizes of fences, shrubs, trees, and all vertical and overhead elements should be planned.

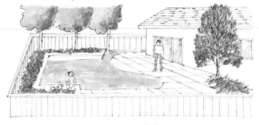

• People's line of vision determines whether a fence provides privacy or merely separation.

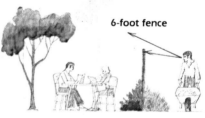

• The purpose for planting a tree determines the kind of tree to be planted—shade trees to walk under, trees for privacy, or decorative trees.

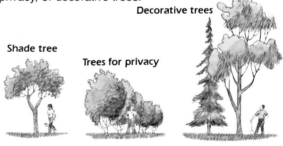

• The purpose for a ground cover or shrub determines the best height for a particular planting: ankle high to cover the ground, knee high for direction, waist high for partial enclosure and traffic control, chest high for division of space, or above eye level for protective enclosure.

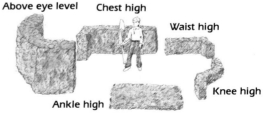

• The easiest flower bed to weed is a raised one with a cap to sit on and a width no greater than a comfortable reach.

• People in motion outdoors require more space than people moving inside a home. Two can walk side by side on a 4-foot garden path, but a 5-foot width gives them more freedom to stroll and raise their eyes from the path.

• People need storage space outdoors. The amount of space required depends on the number and sizes of tools and other items to be stored. You may need to plan storage space for firewood, extra outdoor furniture, games and recreational equipment, a lawn mower, tiki torches, and many other sometimes-used articles.

• Measurement of any equipment people might carry determines the necessary width of gates, passageways, and other openings. The width required for a wheelbarrow extends from a person's knuckle to knuckle, for example, and that required for a clothes basket goes from elbow to elbow.

Knuckle to knuckle

• The normal sitting position of people determines the height of a seat wall or a bench, the depth of a recessed fire pit, and other structural dimensions.

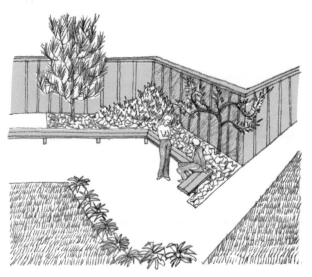

• The amount of space people need for loafing, conversing, or eating will determine the size of a patio, terrace, or deck. Two people sitting on either side of a coffee table take up this much space:

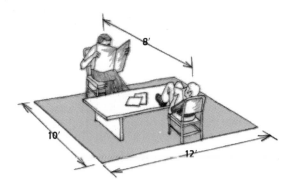

• To establish the dimensions of paved play areas, consider that a tricycle can stay on a 24-inch walk and turn in a 4-foot circle. But three or four children on wheels need space for high-speed turns and races.

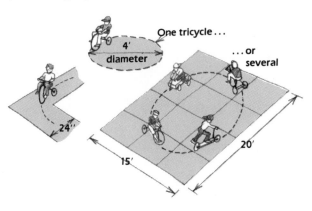

Garden floors:
a step in the right direction

Landscape architects tend to think of gardens in terms of horizontal and vertical planes. And a garden's lowest plane is its floor. A garden floor serves many of the same purposes as the floor of a building, but it offers much more flexibility. Though a garden floor can be paved to make it impervious to water, like a conventional inside floor, it can also be perfectly penetrable, as a lawn is.

Floors from living materials

Materials selected for outdoor floors may be either of two types: plants or building materials. Let's consider plant floors first. Lawns are perhaps the most popular, and for good reason. In the comparatively large areas where they are normally used, they withstand the pressure of many feet and the tumbling of children and pets as no other growing surface can. On the other hand, the dampness of lawn may be a disadvantage if you want a very dry area.

When foot traffic is not a problem, ivy, pachysandra, or various mosses used in the Japanese style can act as close-to-the-earth ground covers and low plane substitutes for lawn.

To create a different effect, you can form part of a garden floor by using a plant that grows to a moderate height. Among the plants in this category are junipers, cotoneasters, and ceanothus.

The French term *parterre de broderie* describes a manner of dressing the ground with a combination of low hedges, gravel, and flowers arranged to form intricate, embroiderylike patterns meant to be observed from above. Patterns from Persian carpets, rya rugs, or even contemporary abstract paintings are means of adapting this method to today's gardens, echoing elaborate 16th century designs.

Water can create still another kind of floor—the surface of a reflecting pond or a swimming pool.

Whatever form of plant material you select for your gar-

(Continued on page 36)

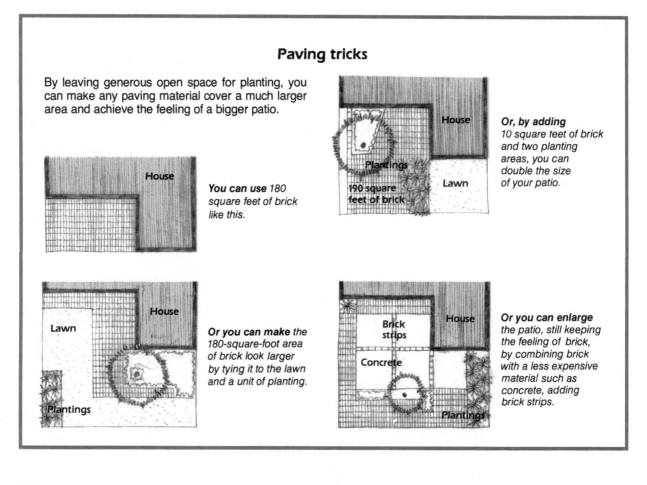

Paving tricks

By leaving generous open space for planting, you can make any paving material cover a much larger area and achieve the feeling of a bigger patio.

You can use 180 square feet of brick like this.

Or, by adding 10 square feet of brick and two planting areas, you can double the size of your patio.

Or you can make the 180-square-foot area of brick look larger by tying it to the lawn and a unit of planting.

Or you can enlarge the patio, still keeping the feeling of brick, by combining brick with a less expensive material such as concrete, adding brick strips.

Nine variations in changing a level

The sketches below show various ways to use steps for changing level in a garden. Note that the different step location and shape set the stage for different outdoor living conditions in each case.

In each scheme, steps not only are an integral part of the garden plan but also have secondary functions—to separate areas, to direct foot traffic, to emphasize a key spot in the garden, to hold back soil, to display plantings, to provide extra seating. In each example the slope has been tailored to fit the stairs, and the shape of the stairs has been varied to meet different needs: for fast or leisurely changes in level, for appearance, for spreading out activities, for making the garden look better.

Narrow steps give upper terrace desired sense of privacy; plantings help muffle noise from play area below.

Living center of garden is reached by corner steps leading from deck to lower level. Citrus trees grow in wood boxes.

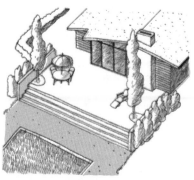

Multiple-duty steps act as retaining wall, facilitate level change, give sense of large-scale dimension.

Broad steps projecting into lower area help tie levels together, especially when activities are spread over both.

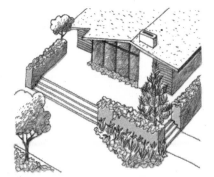

Two sets of steps for different purposes: broad steps lead from living room to garden, narrow ones lead to driveway.

Spacious feeling results from broad, directional steps. Two-level deck breaks space to lower level, joins areas.

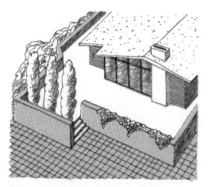

Steps are hidden by low walls to preserve privacy on upper terrace, achieving almost complete isolation.

Level below is enhanced by sweeping, multi-angled steps. Bench seating is provided around tree at deck corner.

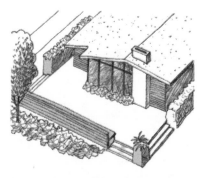

Long, shingle-wall bench serves as retaining wall, matches house siding. Pots on posts emphasize step locations.

den floor, take into account the degree of use you expect the area to receive. Surfaces subject to heavy traffic should be floored with a material that resists abuse. Save delicate ground covers for areas that are more often looked at than trampled on.

Floors from structural materials

In garden areas where heavy-duty floors are needed, you may choose from a broad range of materials. Some kinds of paving—tanbark, gravel, wood decking, and brick-on-sand, for example—allow air and water to percolate through the soil, permitting a healthy growing environment for the roots under these surfaces. At the same time, intense traffic does little or no damage to this type of flooring.

Other pavings that more closely resemble inside floors include concrete and asphalt as well as brick, tile, or flagstone set in mortar. These materials offer many possibilities for durable, decorative floors. In addition, you can combine them or break them into a variety of patterns. Concrete may be colored for a different look. Or you can texture it by exposing its pebbles or by treating it with salt.

You can soften and enrich any paved surface by placing plantings within voids left in the pavement. Though garden paths may be sodded, they are usually paved in order to shed moisture and resist wear. But a flagstone path or terrace with plantings between the stones offers a compromise between naturalness and efficiency that delights the eye.

Similar effects can be gained by use of other materials, such as concrete pads, segregated areas of brick, or—

as is often seen in Japanese gardens—roof tiles set into the pavement.

A garden's horizontal floor plane must often be modified for one reason or another. One vital consideration for any

Cast your own paving blocks *in ground mold: 1) Dig 4-inch mold; 2) Shovel concrete into mold up to rim below grass level; 3) Finish with trowel or wood float; 4) Remember to space for comfortable walking.*

outdoor floor is drainage (see page 47); water must be directed away from living areas and harmlessly dispersed.

Another reason for modifying the garden floor is to create a change of ground level for either practical or esthetic reasons (see page 22). In this case, the floor plan may include retaining walls, as well as ramps or stairs to move people easily from one horizontal plane to another.

For detailed information on garden floors, consult the *Sunset* book *Walks, Walls & Patio Floors.*

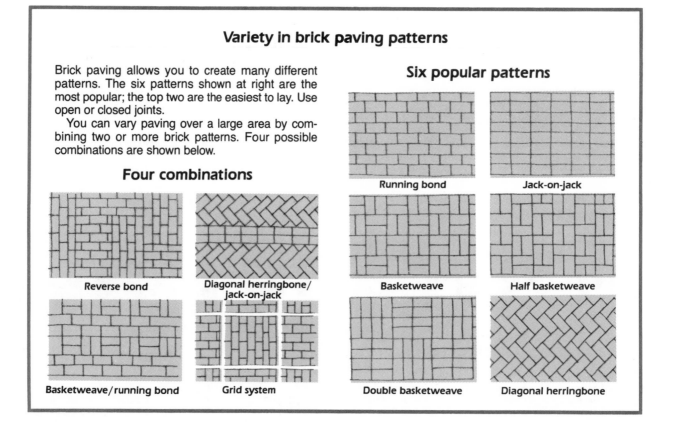

Variety in brick paving patterns

Brick paving allows you to create many different patterns. The six patterns shown at right are the most popular; the top two are the easiest to lay. Use open or closed joints.

You can vary paving over a large area by combining two or more brick patterns. Four possible combinations are shown below.

Four combinations

Reverse bond

Diagonal herringbone/ jack-on-jack

Basketweave/running bond

Grid system

Six popular patterns

Running bond

Jack-on-jack

Basketweave

Half basketweave

Double basketweave

Diagonal herringbone

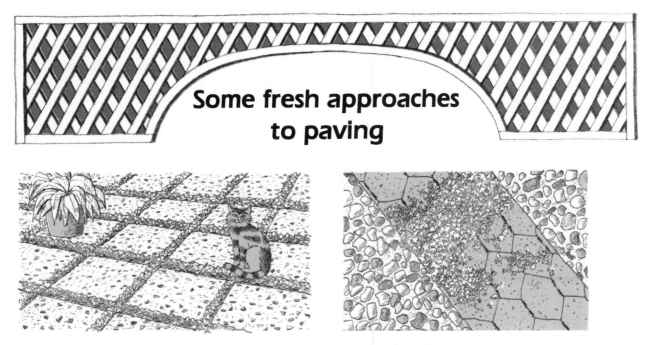

Some fresh approaches to paving

Stepping stones cover old patio

Above left: *Checkerboard of 18-inch-square pebbled stepping stones adds new style to aging concrete patio. The squares are mortared into place, leaving 3-inch spaces between for growing baby's tears (Soleirolia).* **Above right:** *Enlarged view shows how chicken wire is used to hold soil and plants in place. The wire also prevents animals from digging in the spaces. Set chicken wire lower than paving to prevent people from tripping over strips.*

Sledge changes old walk to pathway

Fragments of drab concrete sidewalk can form an attractive garden path. Propping lifted slab on a stone before smashing with sledge prevents shattering into slivers. Fragments are set in 2 inches of sand in 4-inch-deep trench; soil covers sand for later planting.

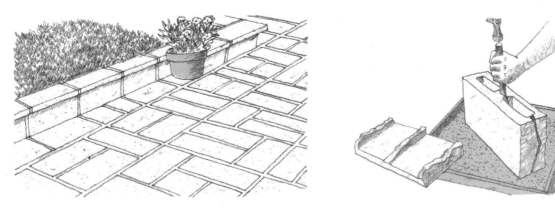

Split block pavement — unusual, inexpensive

Patio in left drawing above is paved with split tan concrete blocks, mortared together ½ inch apart on a 2-inch sand base. Planting beds are bordered with whole blocks set on edge and topped with concrete block caps. Drawing at right shows how to split a block. First, set it on a cushion of sand in a nursery flat. Then firmly tap each partition on both sides of a block with a masonry chisel and hammer. A full split yields two paving rectangles.

Garden walls:
the Chinese had the inspiration

If floors are a garden's lowest horizontal plane, walls provide its chief vertical plane. Sometimes a vertical element is a simple one – the side of a shrub or tree. Sometimes it is more elaborate – a constructed garden wall or the side of a building.

Garden walls can be used to screen off work areas or undesirable views, to provide an enclosure for outdoor dining, to direct the flow of garden traffic, or to form an almost inpenetrable barrier that prevents children or animals from passing through. Walls heighten visual appeal by partitioning off various sections of a garden or by serving as backgrounds to planting beds.

Elliptical doorway *for shady lathhouse stands between 2 by 4 uprights, sits on tapered blocks. Moon gate opening adds appeal to an otherwise conventional garden wall.*

Walls from living materials

Growing walls can take many forms. They may be high or low, or their height may be uneven. You might choose an informal, irregular planting of shrubs or trees—a wall of forsythia, oleander, or roses gives the added pleasure of eye-level blossoms. On the other hand, you might plant a formal, clipped hedge of boxwood or privet. If space is ample and maintenance no problem, one can even create an imposing alleyway of clipped trees, as the gardeners at Versailles did on a large scale.

Walls formed from plant material can be straight or curved, open or dense, solid or penetrable. A growing wall can be deciduous, so that its nature changes with each season.

If you want to divide your yard into separate areas, plants can form a lively screen. A casual line of plants is a far more graceful barrier than a block wall or chain-link fence.

Many flowering shrubs (abelia, diosma, hebe) are adaptable to hedge form. Even formal, seemingly rigid hedges are more dynamic than static, lifeless artificial structures. Hedges of boxwood, syzygium, or holly change from year to year. They possess vents and imperfections that play with moving lights and shadows.

Structures can also be covered with plant materials to create living walls. A vine, such as clematis or morning glory, covering a trellis or solid structure will produce a blaze of vertical color.

Walls from structural materials

Like growing walls, constructed walls can be of any height or of varied heights. But constructed walls have the added advantage of providing for many different textural finishes. They also allow for more security—for example, when a family wants to keep a pet in an enclosed yard.

Constructed walls can be partial (such as a picket fence), solid (a brick wall), translucent (a plastic panel), or even transparent (the space between the rails of a two-rail fence).

Such garden walls often have windows or doors set in them to allow people's vision, people themselves, or vehicles to pass through the walls. Because constructed vertical planes must frequently be penetrable, gates or passageways form an integral part of many walls.

Garden walls may be constructed of many materials. Wooden walls, long-time popular favorites, offer variety ranging from the opacity of board-and-batten fencing to the relative transparency of an arbor's latticework. A garden wall can exude the rustic charm of stone, the richness and texture of brick, the regularity of concrete block, the softness of plaster, the ruggedness of poured concrete, the sparkle of glass, the diffusion of plastic, or the strength of metal.

A wall can be designed in the form of a low bench so that it both defines space and provides convenient seating. Walls may also be designed to retain the earth behind them—a frequent necessity on hillside lots. And many constructed garden walls are adapted to incorporate steps or ramps.

Often a garden wall can be more suggested than actual. For example, a row of trees or posts can create the illusion of a wall; the imagination, prodded by the visual tension, fills in the space between the trees or posts, causing us to accept this space as a solid vertical plane.

The nine drawings on page 35 that illustrate various designs of garden stairs also picture garden walls—some of living materials, some constructed.

Twelve styles of fences

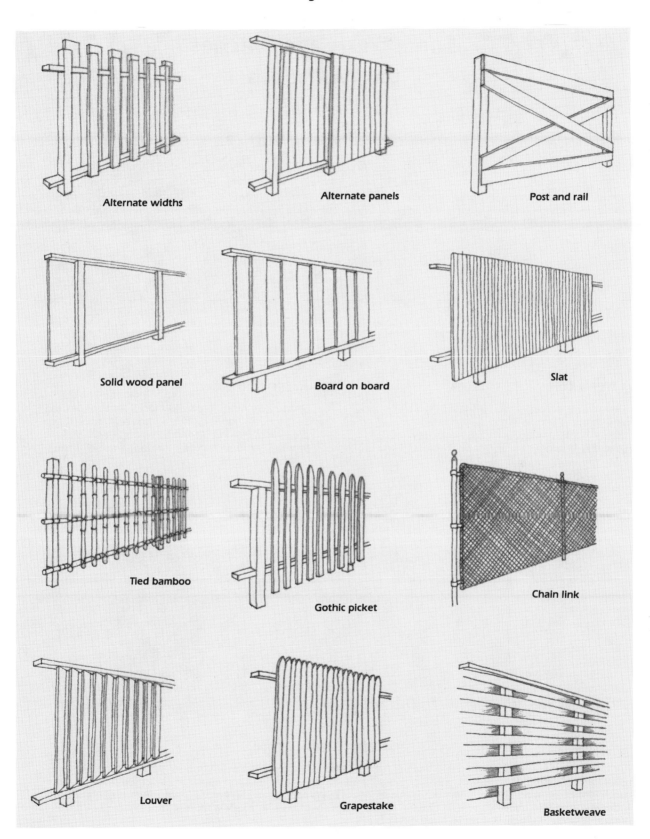

Alternate widths

Alternate panels

Post and rail

Solid wood panel

Board on board

Slat

Tied bamboo

Gothic picket

Chain link

Louver

Grapestake

Basketweave

Some fresh approaches to overheads

A trellis to delight the eye

Brass chains support trellis of 2 by 2s on 2 by 4 frame. Ends are toenailed to house siding for stability; no vertical supports are necessary. Design: Richard A. Wilson.

To block the sun

Decorative, functional trellis blocks some undesired sun, accents opening. This brim keeps sliding glass doors from looking like big holes cut in wall. Trellis provides extra spot to hang a plant. Design: Senna, Kemp, and Kemp.

Strength with grace

Uprights for this ruggedly stylish grape trellis are a quartet of 3 by 3s, bolted at top to notched 3 by 8-inch beams and at bottom to spacer blocks. These are bolted in turn to a metal strap imbedded in a cylindrical concrete pier. Drawing at right shows detail of a corner of the grape arbor. The vertical supports, purposely scaled large to hold up the venerable grape vines, give the structure a light look without sacrificing needed strength. Design: Robert W. Chittock.

Garden ceilings:
put the overhead where it counts

The most common garden ceiling is a limitless one – the sky itself. The old tradition of painting porch ceilings blue to create the illusion of sky suggests the importance of the heavens as a ceiling.

But for a more intimate garden roof, consider the foliage of a spreading tree; the fruits and leaves of an arbor-supported grape vine; canvas, which modifies the intensity of the sun; the shingled wooden roof of a shelter or loggia, which more completely blocks the sun; or many other outdoor ceiling possibilities.

Ceilings from living materials

Creating a garden ceiling with plant materials can be satisfyingly simple: grow a tree to provide a leafy roof, or plant a vine that will fill in an arbor to give overhead shelter.

Trees that will develop spreading canopies over a patio or garden include the silk tree *(Albizia julibrissin),* known as "mimosa" in the eastern United States; coral tree of the *Erythrina* species; goldenrain tree *(Koelreuteria paniculata);* Jerusalem thorn *(Parkinsonia aculeata);* Texas umbrella tree *(Melia azedarach 'Umbraculifera');* and, for the large garden, Southern live oak *(Quercus virginiana).*

Arbor-climbing vines can offer more than mere covering. Many types provide handsome flowers and captivating fragrance. Here are a few:

• For foliage—English ivy *(Hedera helix)* or Boston ivy *(Parthenocissus tricuspidata).*
• For showy flowers—bougainvillea, evergreen clematis *(Clematis armandii),* or Japanese wisteria *(Wisteria floribunda).*
• For fragrance—Carolina jessamine *(Gelsemium sempervirens),* Hall's honeysuckle *(Lonicera japonica* 'Halliana'), or star jasmine *(Trachelospermum jasminoides).*

Like a larger forest, a small grove of trees can give the feeling of a continuous ceiling interrupted by skylights or broken by atriumlike openings where branches spread apart, opening to the sky and letting pools of light fall onto the ground.

Ceilings from structural materials

Roofs for patios and garden structures can be constructed from many different materials. Among the most common are plastic, aluminum, reed or bamboo, canvas, fabric or

Sun shade that grows, *Japanese wisteria provides lavish flower display in early spring, then leafs out in summer.*

metal screening, and glass. In addition, lath, batten, and lumber may be used in such varied ways as solid roofs, louvers, or eggcrate designs.

In choosing the material for an outdoor ceiling, you may select any density from opaque to transparent. Which material you select will depend partly on whether you want to

Overhead frame *with removable lath panels gives shade where you want it. Panels could also be cloth, screening, canvas, or plastic.*

block the sun, rain, or neighbor's view completely, or whether you want to let one or more of those penetrate the space beneath the ceiling. Lattice, for instance, will filter the sun and permit rain to enter. On the other hand, clear glass will intensify the sun's rays, direct the rain away, and give full vision from above.

Garden ceilings may be constructed to fit the existing site, as when a void is left in a ceiling to allow a tree to penetrate. And ceilings need not be built entirely from the same material. A roof area can be partially covered with glass or plastic to allow a limited amount of sun to enter, providing you with a versatile sun-and-shade area.

Though many outdoor ceilings are fixed permanently in position, a movable ceiling can be a great convenience. You can install sliding wood, bamboo, or canvas roof panels that can be adjusted to provide the amount of sun or shade you wish.

For detailed information on garden ceilings, consult the *Sunset* books *Patio Roofs* and *Garden & Patio Building Book.*

Six types of overheads

Canvas

Canvas *will withstand sun, wind, rain. It requires less support and framing than wood but retards air movement.*

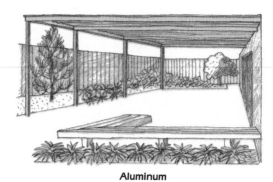

Aluminum

Corrugated aluminum, *available in many colors, blocks all elements; may be noisy in wind, rain.*

Bamboo

Bamboo *provides more densely filtered shade, more natural shade pattern than lath.*

Wood louvers *can be permanent or adjustable – whichever offers better sun control.*

Louver

Fiberglass *is translucent, comes in colors and textures. Material is light, shatter-resistant, easy to work with.*

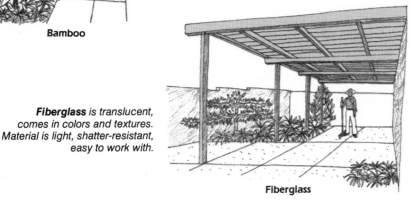

Fiberglass

Lath

Lath, *attractive when vine-covered, filters sun, wind.*

Garden structures:
even adults need playhouses

From the dawn of civilization, people have made efforts to improve their environment. In the process we have invented many kinds of structures – some serving for protection from a harsh climate, others satisfying the need for beauty and entertainment. Traditionally located in gardens, the following structures – or adaptations of them – are very much a part of today's landscaping scene:

• **Houselike structures.** Teahouses, gazebos, poolside shelters, pavilions, private chapels, and temples are among the structures featured in contemporary gardens. The design of such a structure should be compatible with the character of the home that shares its setting. Though a structure need not be in the same style as the house, it should be planned with a comparable scale, texture, proportion, and material in mind.

A freestanding shelter may have the fantasy look of a Victorian valentine, or it might be inspired by the stony and rugged character of an Irish cottage. A shelter may be built of glass and chrome to be slick and shiny, or it may echo the subtle wood tones of a Japanese teahouse. Whatever its style, a shelter should rest comfortably in its setting. Serving as centers of interest, such structures often tempt us into outer reaches of the garden.

• **Arbors and breezeways.** Often these structures form part of a garden by relating one area to another and offering shelter to both people and plants. The more solid and opaque the walls are, the more closely the areas enclosed by arbors and breezeways resemble interior space. The more transparent an arbor is, the more the garden penetrates it and the more it relates to exterior space. Because people react differently to scale in open spaces than in closed ones, relatively open arbor areas should have greater dimensions than relatively closed ones. For example, a person might be quite comfortable in a 10 by 12-foot room but feel cramped on a terrace of the same size.

• **Greenhouses and lath houses.** Though such structures have a primarily practical function, many have been handsomely designed to add grace to the garden. Centuries ago, when a greenhouse was called an orangery, George Washington took great pride in the Georgian elegance of the structure on his Virginia estate. Equally pleasing greenhouses and lath houses can be planned for contemporary gardens.

• **Garden structures that incorporate water.** Water can add a special sparkle to a garden and also provide recreation. A reflecting pond mirrors the sky and the garden scene around it. Fountains add splashes of light and

delightful sounds. Hot tubs and spas encourage soaking both during the day and at night, when bathers can contemplate the shadows cast by the rising moon. And a swimming pool not only offers healthy exercise to both children and adults, but it can also enhance the garden by the special quality of its design.

When a structure containing water is introduced into a garden, it should be appropriate in scope and design to the setting. A swimming pool that resembles a mountain swimming hole would be as out of place on an urban lot as a crisp, chrome-laddered pool would be on a buttercup-carpeted rural meadow. But the possibilities for using water are numerous: in a modest space where even a small fountain might be overpowering, a simple birdbath can add life.

• **Housing for birds and other living creatures.** Animals and insects form an integral part of the garden picture. Beehives are often established in the center of gardens of flowers, from which the bees manufacture their honey. Beautiful dovecotes can be designed to resemble sculptures. Even chickens can be handsomely housed on the periphery of a garden.

• **Fire pits and barbecues.** Providing a convenient means for cooking food outdoors, these garden structures can also serve to raise the temperature of outdoor sitting areas. When not in use, a fire pit can be topped with a wood cover to hold a display of container plants or to

Covered walkway *from house to garage was extended into patio room. Roof of 2 by 6s, 2 by 4s held by 4 by 4 posts. Railing surrounds deck off family room. Design: John Herbst, Jr.*

serve as a low table. Experience has caused many home dwellers to regret building a huge-chimneyed barbecue that, though rarely used, rises to dominate a garden.

• **Structures for children's play.** Here's a type of structure that will allow your imagination free rein. Sandboxes, swings and slides, and playhouses all have their place. But to catch the fancy of growing children, build them a tunnel under an old tree to crawl into, a plastic-covered geodesic dome to climb through, or an elevated tree house for a hideway.

Three ways to garden seating

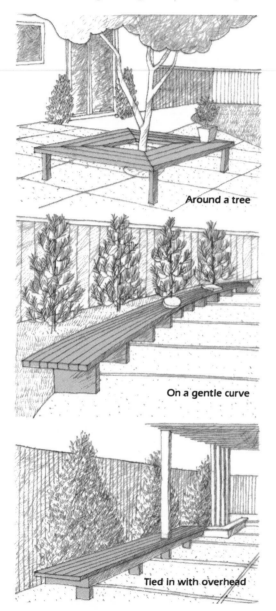

Around a tree

On a gentle curve

Tied in with overhead

For detailed information on garden structures, consult the following *Sunset* books: *Building Barbecues; Children's Rooms & Play Yards; Garden & Patio Building Book; Garden Pools, Fountains & Waterfalls; Patio Book;* and *Swimming Pools.*

Gazebos come in many shapes

Though a gazebo can be one of the most fanciful additions to a garden scene, it can also be one of the most practical.

Think of the many uses such a detached, roofed, and relatively open room can be put to. An entertainment center for formal or buffet dining, a small dancing pavilion, an outdoor reading or sewing room, a game room for children, a dry retreat during a rain storm, a plant shelter—the possibilities multiply.

Pavilion-type gazebo, *complete with flagpole, brings to mind a Sunday afternoon concert in the park.*

Victorian styling *is accentuated by turned posts, ornate shingled roof, lots of gingerbread.*

Redwood gazebo contains a wet bar, porch swing, and lights for night use. Four-inch benderboard forms roof.

Set on single reinforced concrete pier and deck, 13 by 16-foot gazebo seems to float. Design: Earl Powell.

Geodesic dome with triangular windows is versatile gazebo: lath it all, or cover with canvas or plastic.

Let there be light

Garden lighting should be both functional and esthetic. It should illuminate paths, walks, steps, and living areas for use at night, and it should dramatize plant materials.

With the advent of low-voltage systems, outdoor lighting in the garden has become more popular. Low-voltage lighting is safe as long as the connector is properly

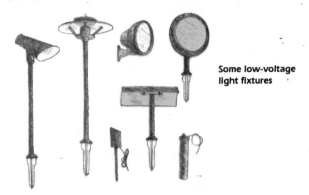

Some low-voltage light fixtures

installed . Even if a child removed the bulb from any 12-volt light fixture and poked a finger inside, there would be little chance of a dangerous electrical shock. If you inadvertently cut a 12-volt cable with a shovel or cultivator, there may be a spark but no shock.

Another important feature of low-voltage lighting is ease of installation. For low-voltage lighting, you need a transformer to reduce your 120-volt household current to the 12-volt current required. Most modern garden light transformers simply plug into any properly installed outdoor outlet. From the transformer on, the 12-volt wiring is simply buried a few inches in the ground, strung along fences, or run up tree trunks—without the need for conduit or protected cable that would be necessary with 120-volt wiring.

You can install low-voltage lighting yourself. If you do not have the time, an electrican can install it throughout your garden at much less cost than 120-volt wiring. And you can easily adjust or move the low-voltage fixtures as your needs change and your plants grow.

Lighting hints

Every garden is different, but here are some factors to keep in mind when you install low-voltage lighting:

• Use six or more small lights throughout your garden rather than two or three more powerful lights.

• Place lights out beyond your patio. They create depth in the garden—and draw insects away from the patio.

• Install separate switches for bright "activity" lights, such as those near a barbecue or table tennis area, so they can be turned off when not needed.

• When hanging lights in trees, place them above the bottom limb to create shadows.

• Be cautious in the use of color filters. A colored light can be handsome in a garden pool or waterfall, but it can destroy the nighttime beauty of flowers, shrubs, and trees.

• Light the hazards as well as the attractions. You know where a garden step is, but guests may not. Use submersible fixtures in wet areas and garden pools, or else waterproof the connections thoroughly with a rubber seam compound. You can place any low-voltage fixture in water, but exposed connections will eventually corrode and fail.

Some fresh approaches to small greenhouses

Become your own nurseryman

A simple starter box like this will allow you to propagate seeds, cuttings. Box is built of redwood, varnished inside and out. Soil is warmed by electrical soil-heating cable set in 2-inch bottom

layer of coarse sand covered with ½-inch hardware cloth. Above that is 6-inch layer of soil, sand, leaf mold, perlite. Box can be put on casters so that it rolls easily to house's north side for summer shade, west side for winter sun.

Kitchen window garden

Inset greenhouse produces herbs for salads, dressings, marinades. Window projects 16 inches from house. Dry vermiculite fills plant box; potted herbs are plunged into it. Hanging pots contain flourishing mint, salad burnet.

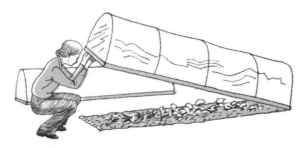

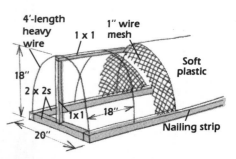

Versatile mini-greenhouse

Not all greenhouses need to be large. Above left is a drawing of a small portable Quonset or oversize cloche. It is 10 feet long and one row wide, weighs 20 pounds. Its basic wire mesh protects plants from marauding animals. In fall, a soft plastic covering laid over the frame shelters seedlings from harsh weather. During hot spells, cheesecloth placed over wire mesh keeps plants from drying out and getting sunburned. Irrigate plants inside cloche by placing soaker hose alongside or by inserting short lengths of plastic pipe under structure's edge. Drawing at right shows dimensions, materials for petite greenhouse.

Drainage – a garden "must"

Few homeowners are versed in the science of hydraulics – handling water in motion. Yet effective drainage control is vital to good garden development.

Why is drainage necessary?

When your neighborhood was still untouched by human hands, chances are that rainwater was absorbed mostly by soil. Now, however, roofs and paved surfaces collect the water and concentrate it in small areas so that the soil can no longer absorb it. The results are runoff, erosion, and flooding.

Even though many lots appear to be level, excavating for a foundation often tilts the soil in one direction or another. During heavy rainstorms, you may discover that water forms pools outside your doors instead of draining away as you would prefer. The steeper the slope, the more critical this aspect of gardening becomes.

Raising a roof is not the only potential source of a drainage problem. You complicate the hydraulics of your lot with each walk, patio, driveway, or other hard surface you install. On hillside lots, drainage becomes all-important

***Neighbors can team up to lick a drainage problem.** Water from several lots collected between two houses (above) and in front garden of one. To make gardens livable, this drainage system collects water from higher lots (rear), channels it between houses through drain of 6-inch agricultural tile set in ditch 2 feet deep. **Below right:** Tile is packed in gravel to 1-foot depth, overlaid with roofing paper to keep out silt. **Below left:** Houses in vicinity of low spot have foundation drains and roof drains tied into a main channel leading to the street. Design: Lawrence Halprin.*

***Downslope runoff** can be handled by gravel-filled surface drain that ties into street storm drain system. Culvert continues drain. Runoff often occurs along driveways.*

when you cut into a natural slope, create a fill by depositing dirt, or remove a slope's native vegetation.

Garden engineering is often a matter of repairing damage. The tasks usually involve hard labor, considerable cost, or both. However, every drain tile, pipe, concrete pour, and piece of lumber may repay you many times over if the result is a garden or a stable slope graced by healthy, attractive plants.

One practical piece of advice about garden engineering: when on your own, tackle only those jobs in which failure brings no serious consequences. If you, as an amateur, attempt major alterations, you may wind up in the worst kinds of legal difficulties with outraged neighbors and with the most expensive kinds of damage to your own house and site. Professional help often pays rich dividends. In any case, always check a major project with your municipal building department before you start.

Types of drains

Conditions on the site or code requirements usually determine which type of drain a homeowner can install.

If the choice is between a drain line leading water off the property and a sump (a dry well), the former is almost always preferable.

Where rainfall occurs in short but violent storms, sumps work well to drain low, boggy spots. But a sump can handle only a limited amount of water; once the soil around it is saturated, it ceases to work at all.

You can create a sump by sinking an 8-foot length of perforated drain tile vertically and filling it with large-mesh rock.

To move water off the property, you can choose between surface and subsurface drains. Surface drains usually take the form of dry streams or flumes. In the past, water was usually not turned loose from a surface drain until its force had been diminished by some device such

Berm at top of slope needn't resemble parking lot curb to do proper job of keeping water off slope. Design: Jocelyn Domela.

as a baffle or sump. However, in some areas the code now allows for water from a surface drain to be spilled directly into the gutter through a break made in the curbing. This avoids the problem of backed-up water in sumps.

Three types of surface drains

At foot of bank, a stream that is dry but decorative in summer, active in winter. Drain line leads from sump.

Brick walk with edges higher than its center carries off downslope surface drainage. Design: A. Arthur Nickman.

Flume needed to drain some banks. This one was made of three 2 by 12s with top grate of 1 by 1s. Design: Jack Littlefield.

Give your garden a touch of drama

Dramatic ... and natural. *Raked ground, flower beds in watering basins characterize Mexican-style garden requiring little water and care – perfect for drought conditions.*

Natives planted *around back patio blend into natural woodland setting. Design: Robert W. Chittock.*

Meticulously manicured *boxwood hedges contribute to formal garden. Flags announce house guests' nationalities. Design: W. David Poot.*

Unmistakably oriental: *koi pool next to kitchen deck. Plantings include grasslike liriope, Japanese pine.*

3. When your yard

Pocket garden attracts attention at steps between lower deck and lawn. Ground cover is baby's tears. Top: dwarf rhododendron; right, woodwardia fern.

Remodeling added sunny lower deck to original shady upper deck, expanding recreational and entertaining possibilities. Steps connect decks; Japanese honeysuckle grows on arbor at right. Design: Josephine C. Willrodt.

needs remodeling

Remodel for a new lease on life

The urge to remodel an older garden may strike for many reasons:

• You buy a house that has been planted by someone whose taste does not match yours.
• After a 3-year try, you decide that your own outdoor efforts leave much to be desired.
• You are struggling with an overgrown, 30-year-old garden, lushly planted but miserly in space.
• The family is growing up. Tricycles have changed to bicycles –or motorbikes. You need a basketball court instead of a sandbox.

Don't resist such reasonable urges to change. Even change for its own sake has rewards.

Doing over the mature garden

Little by little over the years, the domestic jungle closes in. No one knows quite when it happens, but the garden no longer has a place for sunbathing or for growing dahlias, roses, or other sun-loving flowers.

The first step in remodeling such a garden is to move in with saw and pruning shears. Open up shapeless shrubs to get a feeling of their basic framework; yank down tangled vines from arbors. Remove plants that have grown too big for their space.

Whether or not your family includes young children may determine whether or not a plant should stay. Poisonous or thorny plants can present a hazard for children or pets. Plants that bear ornamental fruits often cause stained walks, walls, or interior carpets.

Next, thin out the overhead canopy to allow sunlight to penetrate the trees and give undergrowth a chance to develop.

If you are remodeling an old garden to provide play space for children, don't overlook special opportunities for a tree house, "campsite," or hideout. A private, overgrown path leading nowhere can give children as much pleasure as a jungle gym.

Once you've trimmed your garden back to manageable proportions, you are ready to rearrange traffic patterns, add plants, and build structural elements.

Modifying the unappealing

A bland garden can often be brightened by simple, imaginative touches. A few pot shelves staggered along an expanse of fence will break the monotony. A flowering shrub adds color to a border of all-green shrubs. Such ornamentation as hanging baskets enhances an entryway by making an uninviting roofline more appealing.

When areas are too small, enlarge them. You can often extend lawns, patios, patio overheads, walks, and entry

Problem: *Back yard had no protection from wind, no screening from glare of afternoon sun, no privacy from nearby neighbors.*

Solution: *Lath overhead cuts off neighbor's view, makes outdoor room out of open space. Winds are blocked by glass screen (foreground), plastic panel (beyond lath shelter). Exposed aggregate paving reduces glare. Lath overhead stops short of reaching eaves to keep indoor rooms light.*

Here's what happened...

porches. Adding a section of decking that includes a small hydromassage spa could be a luxurious touch.

A small setback now devoted to lawn could be re-shaped and partially paved to help solve the parking problem. Planting can screen cars from the street or from the house.

Many plants and structures that are basically attractive show off poorly because they are situated badly. Consider grouping similar plants that are set too far apart. Move sun shrubs out of slightly shaded places. Relocate an arbor that casts unwanted shade at the north end of a yard to the yard's south end, where shade is needed.

Concealing the unchangeable

When an unattractive landscape feature can't be altered, you can often hide it from view. Conceal a new stretch of freeway or a neighbor's unkempt yard with fences, free-standing screens, hedges, dense shrubs, or a combina-tion of these elements. The same types of screening can hide service areas, vegetable and cut-flower gardens, and other areas that do not complement the overall land-scape plan.

How about a ground cover to dress up a bank that you thought was too steep to bother with? Or a flowering vine to ramble along a sterile chainlink fence?

Where concrete walkways and patio slabs present a cold look, cover them with wood decking for a warmer appearance.

One particularly common problem is the front face of a house—often a jumble of lines, materials, and staggered windows. A freestanding screen can both hide an undis-tinguished facade and transform wasted public area between street and house into usable private area.

Hide the hose

Three ways to keep a garden hose handy but hidden.

A: In a wall.
Coil hose between studs in 3½ by 13 by 28-inch metal-lined opening.

B: Under a bench. *Hose pushed through opening into box under bench. Faucet hides in fence.*

C: In the ground.
Redwood box, 2 feet square, has hinged lid.

...when two gardens needed a lift

Problem: *Hillside extending too close to home creates an unusable moat only a few feet wide.*

Solution: *Grade was cut back in two levels, creating wide raised planting bed (foreground), broader outdoor living-dining room defined by stone retaining wall. Garage roof extends into upper garden level.*

Before/after remodeling views

Before beginning a landscaping or remodeling project, you need to know how to put garden design to work. These pages show nine ways in which landscaping can give fresh vitality to an older yard.

Here's what remodeling can do for you:

Complement or enhance architecture. Choose plantings to highlight strong building points and tone down weak ones. Here, delicate vertical-character trees contrast with heavy brick steps. A vine softens the entryway arbor; a large background tree relieves the angular lines of the house.

Soften hard architectural lines. The monotonous horizontal line of a fence can be broken by adding well-designed raised planting beds that double as seating. Small trees are planted at regular intervals. Jasmine, grape ivy, and other vines spilling from garden walls also reduce structural rawness, as do junipers sweeping over walkways and tufted grasses rising from patio planting pockets.

Create a study in line. The lines of branch, stem, and leaf draw attention in this closeup garden. Sword-shaped iris leaves, cactus and succulents, the arching stems of abelia and spiraea shrubs, or the winter silhouette of a flowering cherry all provide attractive accents in line.

Serve as a decorative wall. Where a screen or separation of areas is necessary, a row of sheared privet or bay laurel makes a wall seem a far less forbidding barrier. Such flowering shrubs as oleander and flowering leptospermum can take hedge form; they may be tipped back and need not be formally sheared.

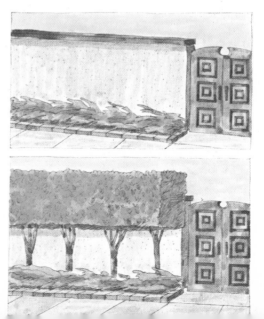

Unify different structural elements. Various manmade structures and disjointed areas within a garden can be tied together effectively with plantings. In this yard, a tunnel-like space between the house and garage has been eliminated by adding a pair of trees and a section of fencing fronted by a narrow garden strip filled with low-growing plants.

Add reflection, shadow, or silhouette. The effect of plants is magnified when they are reflected in a still pool, seen through a translucent panel, or outlined in silhouette against a stark wall. Plants with distinctive forms include Japanese maple, bamboo, and tropical fatsia.

Form a background. This drawing shows a row of large trees—they could be maple or liquidambar—relieving the unbroken flatness of an open patio area. Such dense shrubbery as pittosporum, escallonia, or holly can provide another kind of natural background against which seasonal color can be displayed.

Act as sculpture. Properly pruned, a plant can become a living sculpture. Here a multiple-trunked olive tree makes a strong visual statement along a curved walkway. Sculptural possibilities include specimen plant with interesting branch structure, bonsai, wind-carved tree, or fanciful topiary of boxwood, privet, or yew.

Enframe an area. A semicircle of hedge around this small patio gives a sense of intimacy without complete confinement. This kind of partial screening delineates space without blocking views. Boxwood, dwarf eugenia, and dwarf myrtle enframe well.

Outdoor rooms:
expand your
living space

Outdoor entertaining comes easy on back patio of concrete pads. Design: Lang & Wood.

Classic example of public space reclaimed for private use: Cinderella garden transformed from unused front yard to enclosed courtyard with flower color, trees, benches, fountains, statuary. Design: W. David Poot.

Plant-lined outdoor living/dining room expands home's interior space. Wood pattern adds interest to screened walls. Design: Walt Young.

Glass-roofed dining area, wide container-enlivened patio command view of city skyline, ferry traffic. Design: R. David Adams.

Versailles' Hall of Mirrors may have inspired this garden setting. Garden's length is extended by mirror framed by arbor. Design: Loutrel Briggs.

Round pool, deck, plantings fit compactly into city back yard. Design: Larry Wilson.

Potted red and white geraniums, blue lobelia spark rooftop with color.

City gardens:
urban greening is "in"

Ten floors above street, tiny apartment terrace garden provides leafy, elegant retreat. Design: Wallace Kay Huntington

Partially enframed entertainment area *draws guests together in classic city garden. Design: Thomas Church.*

Smaller party, smaller garden. *Terrace high above Greenwich Village's Christopher Street is made pretty by planting boxes.*

Garden Remodeling
Streetside gardens

Fence enclosing front garden (shown in bottom photo, page 56) eliminates former open lawn. Hollywood junipers stand along fence. Design: W. David Poot.

Colorful burst of pink ivy geranium and roses, yellow calendula sparks streetside view. Tree fern grows roof high.

Elements in front Japanese garden: carpet of Zoysia tenuifolia (Korean grass); lower right, Pittosporum tobira. Espalier is podocarpus. Design: Franz Roubison.

Shallow front public space is enhanced by three carrot wood trees in planting pockets. Design: Galper/Baldon.

When streetside gardens tend to look too much alike, the quickest way to break the uniformity is to use strong vertical elements: hedges, fences, walls, or rows of trees. Combined with planting beds, these elements – arranged high for privacy, low for space division – alter a front yard's look.

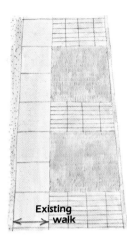

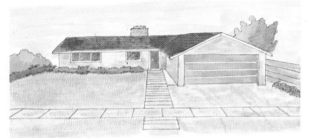

Before: *Conventional streetside planting produces a low-appeal, high-maintenance yard. Large lawn area, exposed front door, narrow walk, bare fence are all drawbacks.*

Style and space both benefit when you alternate two kinds of ground cover.

Brick landing strips punctuate grass parking strip for added interest.

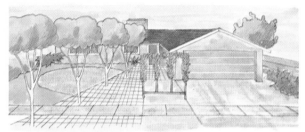

After: *One way to improve yard: Broaden walk, extend row of trees toward house, reduce lawn to semicircle with ground cover, erect trellis to screen entrance.*

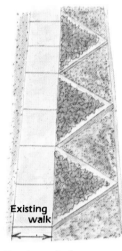

For dynamic lines, header boards separate beds of ground cover, gravel.

Extending concrete to curb with set-in ground cover panels adds pleasing width.

After: *Another remodeling look: Pave lawn area as patio, enclose with vine-covered fence; place stepping stones to new entry court; balance with tree at garage's far side.*

Two ways to dress up a driveway

1. One way to change a driveway's stiff line is to build a raised bed on one side of the drive, balancing it with low plantings on the other side.

2. A more drastic solution: Break up the original walk (save pieces for later use in raised beds); develop a front entry garden with planting beds, paving.

Garden
Remodeling

Hillside sites

Young eucalyptus trees frame beguiling beach view from hillside planted for color. Design: Lang and Wood.

Hillside cutting garden grows in raised planters partially screened from main yard by hedge. Design: R. David Adams.

Dominating lushly planted hillside is orange-flowering Dracaena draco; smaller succulents higher up are Agave attenuata. *White trailing African daisies spill down hill. Design: Lang and Wood.*

Shallow slope

This can be converted with a minimum of grading into a series of level areas. Steps and a raised planting bed serve as low retaining walls. To create a level lawn area in front, the grade has been raised at the street and lowered in front of the house. Two terraces, with both steps and ramp between, take care of the back grade. A tall screen of trees is needed for privacy and wind protection.

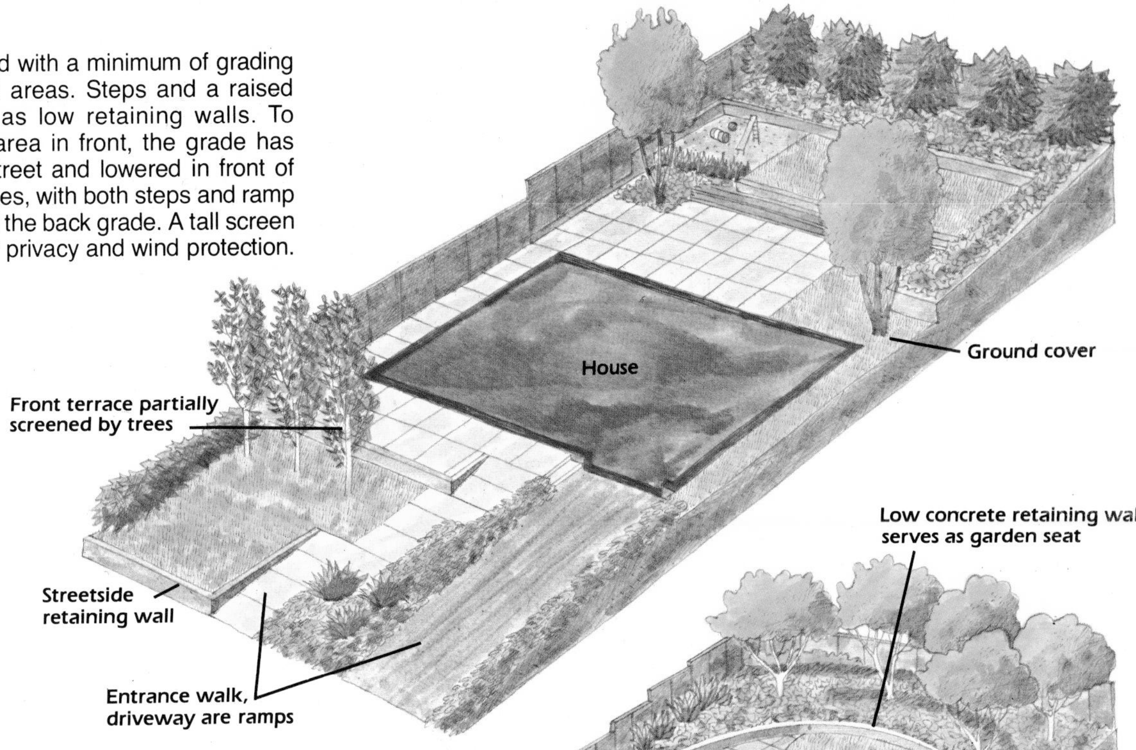

Ground cover

House

Front terrace partially screened by trees

Streetside retaining wall

Entrance walk, driveway are ramps

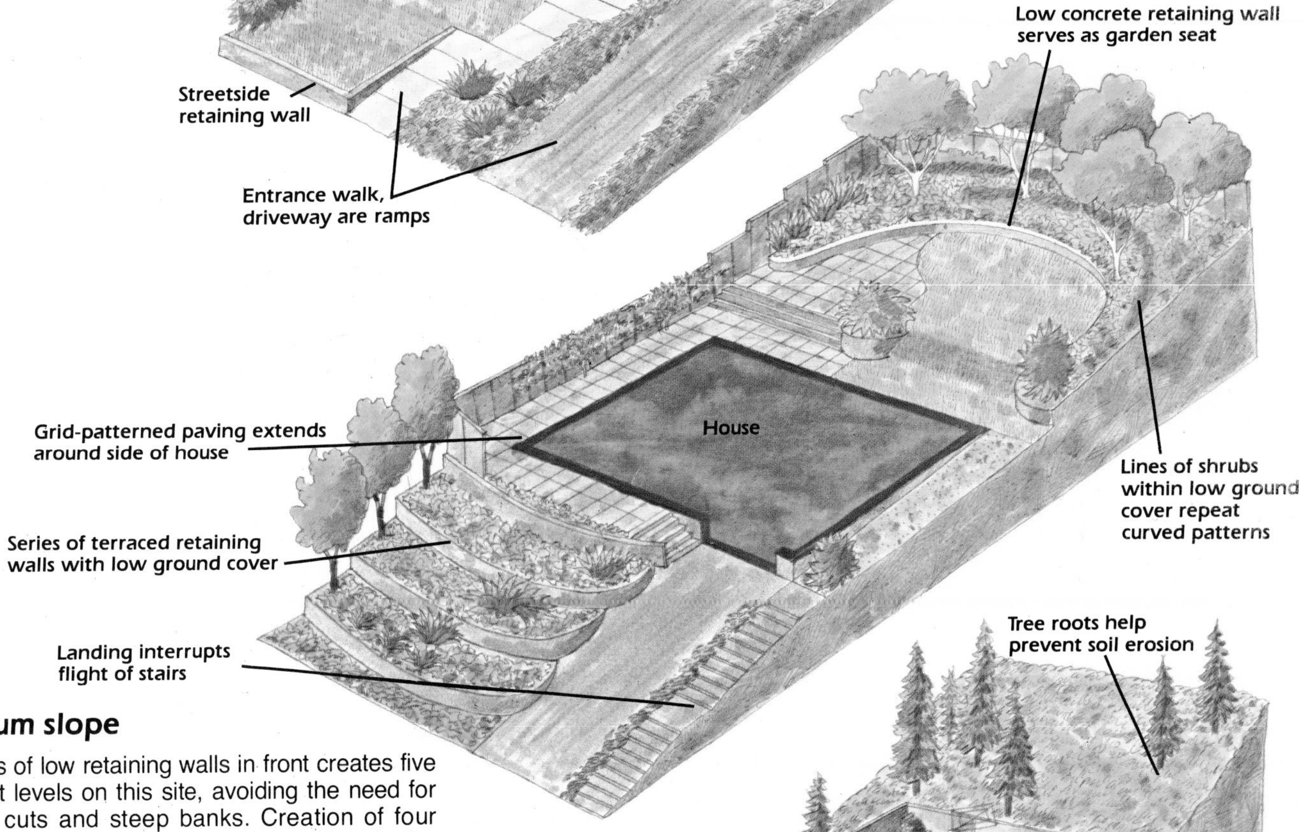

Low concrete retaining wall serves as garden seat

Grid-patterned paving extends around side of house

House

Lines of shrubs within low ground cover repeat curved patterns

Series of terraced retaining walls with low ground cover

Landing interrupts flight of stairs

Medium slope

A series of low retaining walls in front creates five different levels on this site, avoiding the need for radical cuts and steep banks. Creation of four sweeping levels solved the slope problem in the rear yard. Note that the back lawn ramps down so that the mower need not be lifted or pulled up and down stairs.

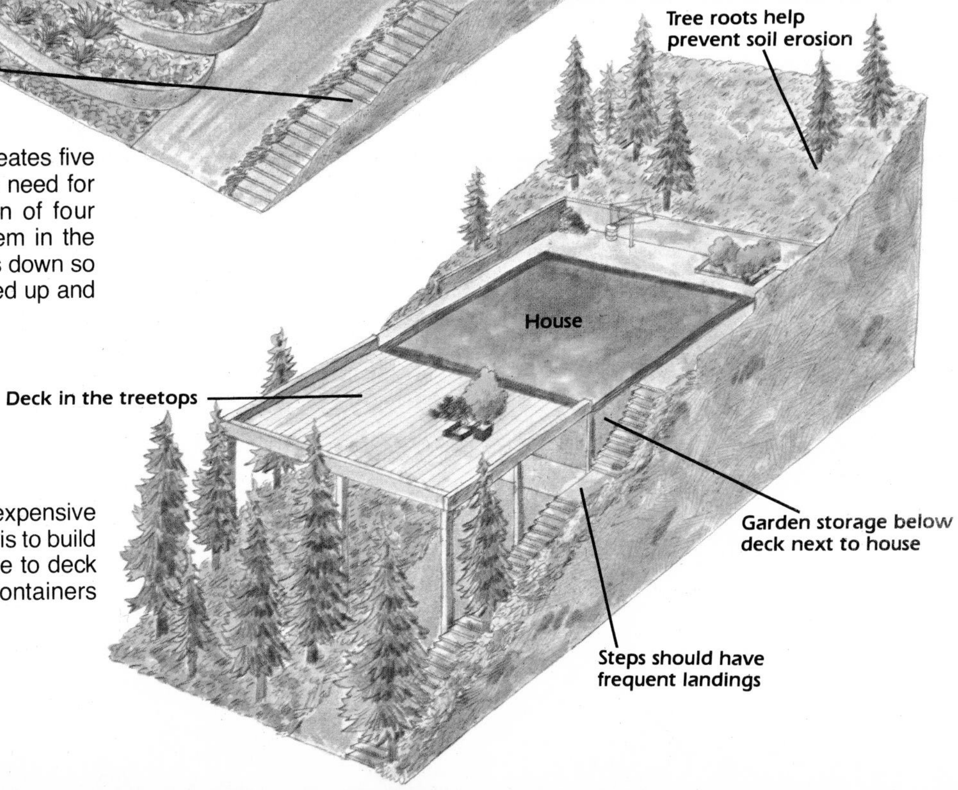

Tree roots help prevent soil erosion

House

Deck in the treetops

Steep slope

In many cases, the simplest and least expensive way to provide level space on a steep lot is to build a deck. A tree planting that brings foliage to deck height lessens the perched feeling. Containers permit gardening on the deck.

Garden storage below deck next to house

Steps should have frequent landings

Garden Remodeling

Children's play yards

Sandbox area (foreground), play equipment (background) are ringed by cement walk that doubles as racetrack for bicycles, small vehicles. Design: Jones/Peterson.

Stylish play yard combines slide, playhouse, sand-filled area. Tree stumps outline yard. Design: Walt Young.

Outgrown sandbox is covered by decking built around inviting hot tub.

Outdoor spa's refreshing waters attract frolicking children. Tiled pool and wall base, inset stained glass panels, potted plants add color. Design: Dagmar Braun.

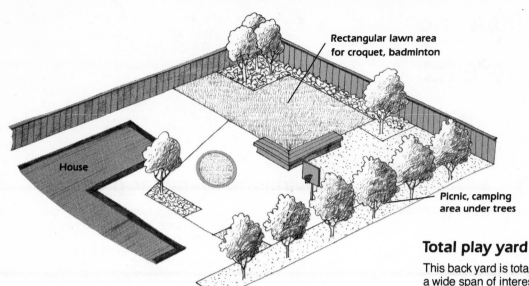

Rectangular lawn area
for croquet, badminton

House

Picnic, camping
area under trees

Total play yard

This back yard is totally given over to recreation for a wide span of interests and ages: 1) Lawn for croquet, badminton, and "camping out"; 2) Tanbark play area; 3) Asphalt for basketball and wheel toys; 4) Sandbox; 5) Small circular lawn for fire pit.

Lawn panel serves
same purpose as
playroom rug

House

Raised bed protects
plants, offers seating

Low-care play yard

The simple design of this yard avoids confusion and minimizes maintenance. Asphalt paving, carried to the fence, gives a large and interesting area for wheel toys. The raised planting bed protects the flower border from traffic. A generous cap around the pentagonal sandbox provides for seating in all directions.

House

Angled deck increases
apparent rear yard space

All-weather play yard

Here is a playroom protected from rain and sun. Half the deck is roofed solid; half is sheltered only by a vine-covered trellis. A seat fixed to the roof posts serves both to rail the far edge of the deck and to provide seating along the deck's entire width. Canvas along the roof edge rolls down on rainy days.

Garden Remodeling 65

Garden Remodeling
Parking areas

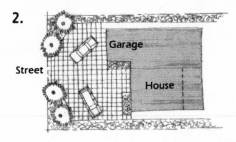

2.

The auto is a space eater. Though the car itself covers only 100 square feet or so, it needs several times this much room to back and turn around; its doors must open; it shouldn't come too close to a wall or a paving edge. All of this makes car circulation, car parking, and car storage most difficult on a small lot.

What are your choices?

If your street frontage is 75 feet or less and if you would like the conveniences of off-street parking and the shortest possible walk from car to house, then you have only a few good choices. In many subdivisions you are handed this situation.

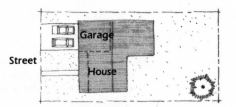

Your garage gives you covered storage for two cars. Your driveway gives you off-street parking for two more cars, but you lack a pleasant arrival court. You pave much of your front yard, but you get limited benefit from it. The stiff lines of your driveway and entry walk are ho-hum repetitions of the paving lines of your neighbors.

What can you do? Here are two answers, both variations of the entry court or arrival court.

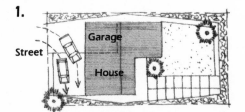

1.

In the plan shown above, you pave part of your front yard as you would a patio, and screen this paving from the street with planting.

Following is a more informal arrangement, in which you remove your old driveway and replace it with a larger motor court. The surface could be conventional asphalt or concrete set off in grids. Or you could use tile or brick, or even crushed granite or gravel.

Solving the cul-de-sac problem

If you live on a conventional straight street, you may have all the guest parking you need freely available to you. But on a cul-de-sac, this may not be true.

In a cul-de-sac situation, all lots taper toward the street, with the result that there isn't always room for a car between driveways. Five lots, for example, might provide street parking for only four cars; on a straight street there would be room for six or eight on each side of the street. The answer here? Sometimes a motor court like this one:

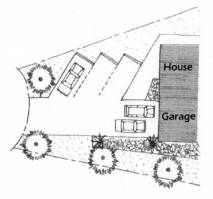

Here one side of the tapered front yard contains front lawn and trees, the other side a guest parking court with space for three cars clearly indicated by header strips in the paving and wheel stops at the end of each parking bay.

Check your remodeling plans with the local inspector for compliance with the off-street parking code.

Where there are no sidewalks

The following solution works well in suburban areas without sidewalks. Essentially, the idea is simply angle parking, the space saver used by many cities, but here it is combined with attractive plantings.

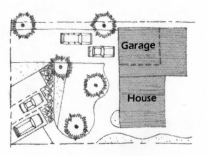

4. Selecting your basic plants

In planning a new garden or remodeling an old one, you will want to establish a permanent planting framework—one that will be independent of the come and go of seasonal color.

Twelve pages of charts

The charts on the following pages are a guide to selecting plants for your garden framework. Plants are divided into six functional groups: small and medium-size trees; hedges, screens, and borders; basic shrubs; ground covers; vines; and plants to cascade over a wall. The plants you'll find were chosen not necessarily for their individual qualities but for their effectiveness when used in combination with other plants.

You will want to choose plants that will be attractive to you throughout the year, regardless of how their appearance may change with the seasons. You will want plants that are well adapted to your climate, exposure, and soil conditions. Temperamental and tender plants should play secondary roles in your landscape scheme so that their loss would not destroy the garden framework you have established.

Remember to build the basic planting framework with simplicity. Everything you do with plants that have strong character or structure—or with seasonal color in bulbs, annuals, perennials, roses, or other favorites—will be more telling because of this simple background.

Plant hardiness zone map

The plant hardiness zone map below—devised by the United States Department of Agriculture—is used in countless nursery catalogs and garden books to indicate where plants can be grown. In the map's original concept, readers were to locate on the map the climate zone in which they lived; then, if the zone number given for a particular plant was the same as, or smaller than, their climate zone number, the plant was judged to be hardy in their locale. In our listings, we have followed the standard method of hardiness rating; but in addition to indicating the coldest zone the plant will grow in, we consider its adaptability and usefulness in the warmer zones, and indicate all zones in which the plant is generally grown.

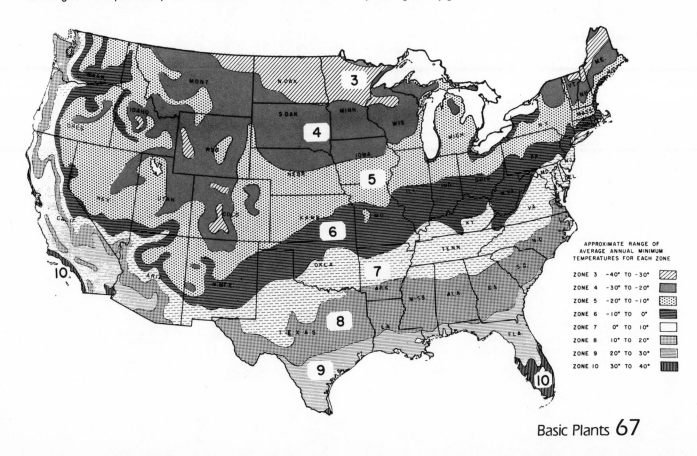

APPROXIMATE RANGE OF AVERAGE ANNUAL MINIMUM TEMPERATURES FOR EACH ZONE

ZONE 3 −40° TO −30°
ZONE 4 −30° TO −20°
ZONE 5 −20° TO −10°
ZONE 6 −10° TO 0°
ZONE 7 0° TO 10°
ZONE 8 10° TO 20°
ZONE 9 20° TO 30°
ZONE 10 30° TO 40°

NAME OF PLANT	EVERGREEN OR DECIDUOUS	FLOWERS	ATTRACTIVE FRUIT	DISTINCTIVE FOLIAGE	SHADE	PATIO TREE	CLIMATE ZONES								REMARKS
							3	4	5	6	7	8	9	10	
Acer ginnala AMUR MAPLE	D					•	•	•	•	•	•	•	•		Grown as a single tree or multiple trunked tall shrub.
A. palmatum JAPANESE MAPLE	D			•		•				•	•	•	•		Slow growth to 20 feet. Normally many stemmed, but can be trained as single tree.
Albizia julibrissin SILK TREE	D	•			•	•					•	•	•	•	Makes a beautiful canopy.
Amelanchier laevis SHADBUSH	D	•	•			•		•	•	•	•	•			White flowers in long drooping clusters before the leaves in early spring.
Arbutus unedo STRAWBERRY TREE	E	•	•	•		•						•	•	•	Attractive red brown, shreddy bark.
Betula pendula EUROPEAN WHITE BIRCH	D					•	•	•	•	•	•	•	•	•	Often sold as *B. alba* or *B. pendula*. Suitable for grove planting.
Cercidiphyllum japonicum KATSURA TREE	D			•	•				•	•	•	•	•		Light and dainty branch and leaf pattern. Single or multiple trunk.
Cercis canadensis EASTERN REDBUD	D	•		•		•			•	•	•	•	•		Profusion of small rosy pink flowers on bare twigs in spring. Excellent fall color.
Chionanthus virginicus FRINGE TREE	D	•				•			•	•	•	•			White flowers in lacy clusters. Deep yellow fall color.
Cladrastis lutea YELLOW WOOD	D	•				•	•	•	•	•	•	•			Leaves look somewhat like English walnut, bright green. Brilliant yellow in fall.
Cornus florida FLOWERING DOGWOOD	D	•				•			•	•	•	•	•		*C. f.* 'Rubra' is a longtime favorite for its pink or rose bracts. 'Cherokee Chief' has deep rosy red bracts that are paler at base.
C. kousa KOUSA DOGWOOD	D	•	•	•							•	•	•	•	Delicate limb structure and dense, spreading horizontal growth habit.
Crataegus lavallei LAVALLE HAWTHORN	D	•	•	•					•	•	•	•	•		More erect and open branching with less twiggy growth than other hawthorns. White flowers. Large orange or red fruits.
C. oxyacantha ENGLISH HAWTHORN	D	•	•		•				•	•	•	•			Best known through its varieties: 'Paul's Scarlet', double rose to red flowers; 'Double White', 'Double Pink'.
C. phaenopyrum WASHINGTON THORN	D	•	•		•	•			•	•	•	•	•		More graceful and delicate than other hawthorns. White flowers. Chinese red fruits in autumn.
Cydonia oblonga FRUITING QUINCE	D	•	•	•		•					•	•	•	•	Yellow fruit and fall foliage. Will tolerate wet soil.
Diospyros kaki ORIENTAL or JAPANESE PERSIMMON	D		•	•		•							•	•	Spectacular large orange fruits hang on after leaves fall.
Elaeagnus angustifolia RUSSIAN OLIVE	D			•	•		•	•	•	•	•	•	•		Takes any soil. When pruned and trained makes picturesque tree.
Eriobotrya deflexa BRONZE LOQUAT	E		•			•						•	•	•	Bronze color of new growth lasts long before turning dark green.
E. japonica LOQUAT	E		•	•		•						•	•	•	Lawn or patio. Prune to shape. Big leathery leaves. Orange to yellow fruits.
Ginkgo biloba MAIDENHAIR TREE	D			•	•	•					•	•	•	•	Excellent yellow fall color. Plant only male trees.
Gleditsia triacanthos inermis HONEY LOCUST	D				•						•	•	•	•	Leaves come out late, drop early. Several varieties, all thornless.
Halesia carolina SNOWDROP TREE	D	•	•			•				•	•	•	•	•	Grows 25-30 feet. Good overhead planting for azaleas and rhododendrons.

NAME OF PLANT	EVERGREEN OR DECIDUOUS	FLOWERS	ATTRACTIVE FRUIT	DISTINCTIVE FOLIAGE	SHADE	PATIO TREE	CLIMATE ZONES								REMARKS
							3	4	5	6	7	8	9	10	
Ilex altaclarensis 'Wilsonli' WILSON HOLLY	E		•			•				•	•	•	•		Shrub trained as small tree.
I. opaca AMERICAN HOLLY	E		•			•			•	•	•	•	•		Many selected forms.
Koelreuteria paniculata GOLDENRAIN TREE	D	•	•		•	•			•	•	•	•	•		Yellow flowers in upright clusters in summer. Bladderlike pods in fall.
Laburnum watereri 'Vossii' GOLDENCHAIN TREE	D	•				•			•	•	•	•	•		Yellow flower clusters 10-20 inches long.
Lagerstroemia indica CRAPE MYRTLE	D	•				•					•	•	•		White, pink, red, lavender varieties. Available in shrub or tree form.
Ligustrum lucidum GLOSSY PRIVET	E			•	•	•					•	•	•	•	Round headed when trained to single trunk.
Magnolia grandiflora 'St. Mary' ST. MARY MAGNOLIA	E	•	•	•		•					•	•	•	•	Compact form of southern magnolia.
M. soulangiana SAUCER MAGNOLIA	D	•				•			•	•	•	•	•	•	To 25 feet when trained as a tree.
Malus CRABAPPLE	D	•				•		•	•	•	•	•			Many kinds varying in size, color, and hardiness.
Nerium oleander OLEANDER	E	•				•						•	•	•	Needs training to become single-trunk tree, and constant sucker removal to remain one.
Nyssa sylvatica SOUR GUM, TUPELO	D		•		•	•			•	•	•	•	•		Copper red fall color, picturesque out of leaf. Very adaptable.
Olea europaea OLIVE	E			•		•							•	•	Willowlike gray green leaves. Best as multiple-trunked tree.
Oxydendrum arboreum SOURWOOD, SORREL TREE	D	•		•	•	•				•	•	•	•		Avoid underplanting with anything needing cultivation.
Pistacia chinensis CHINESE PISTACHE	D		•	•	•	•							•	•	Fall color in red tones. Not fussy about soil, water.
Pittosporum rhombifolium QUEENSLAND PITTOSPORUM	E		•	•		•							•	•	Very showy yellow to orange fruits and glossy, diamond-shaped leaves.
Prunus FLOWERING CHERRY	D	•							•	•	•	•	•		Many kinds are sold which differ in growth habit, flower color.
Prunus blireiana BLIREIANA PLUM	D	•			•	•			•	•	•	•	•		Graceful. Leaves reddish purple, turning greenish bronze in summer. No fruits.
Prunus cerasifera 'Atropurpurea' PURPLE-LEAF PLUM	D	•		•	•	•		•	•	•	•	•	•		White flowers are followed by bronzy purple leaves. Fast growing.
P. c. 'Newport' PURPLE-LEAF PLUM	D	•	•			•		•	•	•	•	•	•		Purplish red leaves. Single pink flowers. Will bear a few fruits.
P. c. 'Thundercloud' THUNDERCLOUD PLUM	D	•	•			•		•	•	•	•	•	•		Dark coppery leaves. Flowers light pink to white. Sometimes sets good fruit crop.
Pyrus kawakamii EVERGREEN PEAR	E	•		•		•							•	•	Needs training to become a single-trunked tree.
Sophora japonica JAPANESE PAGODA TREE, CHINESE SCHOLAR TREE	D	•			•	•			•	•	•	•	•	•	Spreading tree, not particular about soil or water.
Sorbus aucuparia EUROPEAN MOUNTAIN ASH	D	•	•		•		•	•	•	•	•	•			Clusters of white flowers in late spring followed by clusters of bright orange-red "berries."
Styrax japonica JAPANESE SNOWBELL	D	•				•			•	•	•	•	•		Leaves angle upward from branches, white flowers hang down, giving parallel tiers of green and white.

NAME OF PLANT	EVERGREEN OR DECIDUOUS	UNDER 3 FT.	3 TO 6 FT.	6 TO 12 FT.	OVER 12 FT.	MAY BE SHEARED	CLIMATE ZONES 3	4	5	6	7	8	9	10	REMARKS
Abelia grandiflora GLOSSY ABELIA	E		•			•				•	•	•	•	•	Treat as perennial in coldest areas.
Acer campestre HEDGE MAPLE	D			•	•			•	•	•	•	•			Dense foliage; compact when clipped.
A. saccharum 'Monumentale' SENTRY MAPLE	D				•				•	•	•	•			Columnar. Plant close for 20-foot-high screen.
BAMBOO	E	•	•	•	•						•	•	•	•	Choose from many. Vary in hardiness and height from 1½ to 50 feet. Yellow groove bamboo (*Phyllostachys aureosulcata*) is hardy to −20°.
Berberis buxifolia 'Nana' DWARF MAGELLAN BARBERRY	E	•				•				•	•	•	•		1½ feet high, 2½ feet wide. Good show of yellow flowers if not sheared.
B. julianae WINTERGREEN BARBERRY	Semi E		•			•			•	•	•	•			Hollylike, leathery dark green leaves. Very thorny. Good barrier. Can be held to 3 feet.
B. mentorensis MENTOR BARBERRY	Semi E		•			•			•	•	•	•			Compact growth. Dull dark red berries. Stands hot midwest summers.
B. thunbergii JAPANESE BARBERRY	D		•			•			•	•	•	•	•		Dense foliage. Bright red berries. Also red leaf and dwarf varieties.
Buxus microphylla japonica JAPANESE BOXWOOD	E	•	•			•				•	•	•			Tolerates hot summers. Poor appearance in cold winters.
B. m. koreana KOREAN BOXWOOD	E	•				•			•	•	•				Slower and lower growing than Japanese boxwood. Hardy to −18°.
B. sempervirens COMMON BOXWOOD	E					•				•	•	•			Generally clipped to 3 to 5 feet but will reach 15 feet or more if not pruned.
B. s. 'Suffruticosa' TRUE DWARF BOXWOOD	E	•				•				•	•	•	•		Slow growing. Small leaves, dense form.
CAMELLIA	E		•								•	•	•	•	Choose vigorous upright growing varieties. Hybrid 'Flirtation' will take full sun.
Cotoneaster divaricatus SPREADING COTONEASTER	D	•	•			•				•	•	•			Most often recommended for shrub border. Pink flowers give way to red fruit.
Cupressus glabra ARIZONA CYPRESS	E			•		•					•	•	•		Takes dry, hot situations.
Deutzia gracilis SLENDER DEUTZIA	D	•							•	•	•	•			One of the best dwarf shrubs.
Dodonaea viscosa HOP BUSH, HOPSEED BUSH	E			•								•	•	•	Takes any kind of soil, ocean wind, desert heat. There also is a purple-leafed variety.
Elaeagnus angustifolia RUSSIAN OLIVE	D			•	•		•	•	•	•	•	•			Gray foliage. Thrives in any soil, nearly every climate.
E. pungens 'Fruitlandii' FRUITLAND SILVERBERRY	E			•		•						•	•	•	Especially valuable for seashore plantings. Silvery foliage.
EUONYMUS	E	•				•					•	•	•		Several varieties of *E. japonica* and *E. kioutschovica* are useful as hedges.
E. alata 'Compacta' DWARF WINGED EUONYMUS	D	•				•			•	•	•	•			Best when unclipped. Rich rose red fall color.
E. japonica 'Microphylla' BOX-LEAF EUONYMUS	E	•				•				•	•	•	•		Small leaves, compact growth, 1 to 2 feet tall and half as wide. Excellent edger.

NAME OF PLANT	EVERGREEN OR DECIDUOUS	UNDER 3 FT.	3 TO 6 FT.	6 TO 12 FT.	OVER 12 FT.	MAY BE SHEARED	CLIMATE ZONES								REMARKS
							3	4	5	6	7	8	9	10	
Feijoa sellowiana PINEAPPLE GUAVA	E			•	•	•						•	•	•	Gray green foliage. Exotic fruit.
Gardenia jasminoides	E	•	•									•	•	•	Subject to periodic cold damage.
Hakea laurina SEA URCHIN, PINCUSHION TREE	E			•	•								•	•	Dense plant with narrow, gray green leaves.
H. suaveolens SWEET HAKEA	E			•	•								•	•	Stiff needlelike leaves are stickery. Makes good barrier.
Hypericum patulum 'Hidcote'	Semi E	•				•					•	•	•		Deciduous in zone 7. Yellow flowers are 3 inches across.
Ilex cornuta CHINESE HOLLY	E		•	•		•					•	•	•	•	Without pruning, will grow to 10 feet. 'Burfordii' is the favorite variety.
I. crenata JAPANESE HOLLY	E	•	•	•	•	•				•	•	•	•		Looks more like boxwood than holly. Will grow to 20 feet. Many varieties.
I. glabra INKBERRY	E	•	•	•	•	•			•	•	•	•	•		Boxwoodlike leaves. Low hedge or border. Dense. Slow growing. Hardy native.
I. opaca AMERICAN HOLLY	E		•	•	•	•			•	•	•	•	•		'Clarke', 'David', and 'Hedgeholly' are good varieties for hedges and screens.
I. vomitoria YAUPON	E	•	•	•	•	•				•	•	•	•		Accepts both seashore and dry interior conditions. 'Nana' is an excellent dwarf form.
Laurus nobilis GRECIAN LAUREL	E			•	•						•	•	•		Slow growing. Good container shrub.
Ligustrum amurense AMUR RIVER PRIVET	D		•	•	•	•			•	•	•	•	•	•	Hardiest of the semievergreen privets.
L. japonicum JAPANESE PRIVET	E		•	•	•						•	•	•	•	Bushier and more shrublike than *L. lucidum*.
L. lucidum GLOSSY PRIVET	E		•	•	•						•	•	•	•	Larger leaves than Japanese privet. Can be grown as small tree. Tall screen.
L. ovalifolium CALIFORNIA PRIVET	Semi E	•	•	•	•						•	•	•	•	Widely planted. Evergreen only in mild climates.
L. 'Vicaryi' VICARY GOLDEN PRIVET	E	•	•			•					•	•	•	•	Evergreen in warm areas. Dwarf growing. Bright golden foliage all year.
Liquidambar styraciflua AMERICAN SWEET GUM	D			•	•					•	•	•	•	•	Plant 6 feet apart.
Lonicera tatarica TARTARIAN HONEYSUCKLE	D		•				•	•	•	•	•	•	•		Many varieties, pink to white. Plant 5 feet apart for screen.
Myrsine africana AFRICAN BOXWOOD	E	•	•			•						•	•	•	Red stems, tiny boxwoodlike foliage. Good for clipped hedges.
Myrtus communis TRUE MYRTLE	E	•	•			•						•	•		Dwarf form most frequently used as low hedge.
Nerium oleander OLEANDER	E		•	•	•						•	•	•	•	Many colors. Wide spreading unless clipped.
Osmanthus fragrans SWEET OLIVE	E		•	•	•								•	•	Fragrant but inconspicuous flowers. A tradition for Southern gardens.
O. heterophyllus HOLLY-LEAF OSMANTHUS	E		•	•		•					•	•	•	•	Several varieties. 'Gulftide' has glossy dark green foliage.
Philadelphus virginalis MOCK ORANGE	D		•						•	•	•	•			Double white flowers.

NAME OF PLANT	EVERGREEN OR DECIDUOUS	UNDER 3 FT.	3 TO 6 FT.	6 TO 12 FT.	OVER 12 FT.	MAY BE SHEARED	CLIMATE ZONES								REMARKS
							3	4	5	6	7	8	9	10	
Photinia fraseri	E				•	•					•	•	•	•	New growth coppery red.
P. serrulata CHINESE PHOTINIA	E				•	•					•	•	•	•	New growth bronzy.
Pieris japonica LILY-OF-THE-VALLEY SHRUB	E	•	•			•			•	•	•	•	•		Requires acid soil. Protect from sun and wind.
Pinus nigra AUSTRIAN BLACK PINE	E			•				•	•	•	•	•			Also windbreak. Dark green glossy foliage with very stiff needles.
P. resinosa RED PINE	E			•				•	•	•	•	•			Very hardy native. Dark green, flexible needles 4 to 6 inches long.
Pittosporum eugenioides	E		•	•	•								•	•	Glossy leaves have distinctive wavy edges.
P. tobira TOBIRA	E		•	•	•	•						•	•	•	Leathery leaves in whorls. A choice variegated form is available.
Podocarpus macrophyllus YEW PINE	E			•	•							•	•	•	Beautiful sheared screen.
Prunus caroliniana CAROLINA CHERRY LAUREL	E		•	•	•	•					•	•	•	•	Attractive foliage.
P. laurocerasus ENGLISH LAUREL	E			•	•	•					•	•	•		Heavy, rich green foliage.
Pyracantha coccinea FIRETHORN	E		•	•		•				•	•	•	•	•	Many varieties.
Rhamnus frangula 'Columnaris' TALLHEDGE BUCKTHORN	D		•			•			•	•	•	•			Set 2½ feet apart for a tight narrow hedge or screen. Can be held to 4 feet.
Salix purpurea 'Gracilis' DWARF PURPLE OSIER	D	•				•		•	•	•	•	•			Fine texture, blue gray color effect. Can be kept at 1 foot high and as wide.
Santolina chamaecyparissus LAVENDER COTTON	E	•				•						•	•	•	Plant 2 feet apart for edgings and borders. Clip to 1 foot to keep neat. Gray foliage. Yellow button flowers.
Spiraea bumalda 'Anthony Waterer' DWARF RED SPIRAEA	D	•							•	•	•	•	•		Dwarf to 1½ feet or less. Makes low hedge or border.
S. vanhouttei BRIDAL WREATH	D		•						•	•	•	•	•		White flowers in summer. Fast growing.
Taxus cuspidata JAPANESE YEW	E		•	•		•		•	•	•	•	•	•		Many varieties.
T. c. 'Nana' DWARF JAPANESE YEW	E	•						•	•	•	•	•	•		Shrubby, spreading wider than high. Under 1½ feet.
T. media 'Hicksii'	E		•			•		•	•	•	•	•	•		Columnar.
Teucrium chamaedrys	E	•				•			•	•	•	•	•	•	Can be clipped any height up to 12 inches.
Thuja occidentalis 'Douglas Pyramidal' AMERICAN ARBORVITAE	E		•	•	•		•	•	•	•	•	•	•		Grows 8 to 15 feet.
Tsuga canadensis CANADA HEMLOCK	E		•	•	•		•	•	•	•	•	•	•		Prune and shear to any shape and height.
T. caroliniana CAROLINA HEMLOCK	E		•	•	•			•	•	•	•	•	•		Similar to above.
Viburnum opulus 'Nanum'	D	•				•		•	•	•	•	•	•	•	Highly regarded in cold areas.
Xylosma congestum	E-D		•	•	•							•	•	•	Height is easily controlled. May lose all leaves after sharp frost.

Basic shrubs

NAME OF PLANT	EVERGREEN OR DECIDUOUS	LESS THAN 3 FT.	3 TO 5 FT.	5 TO 8 FT.	CLIMATE ZONES								REMARKS
					3	4	5	6	7	8	9	10	
Aucuba japonica JAPANESE AUCUBA	E			•					•	•	•	•	Many variegated forms are available.
Berberis verruculosa WARTY BARBERRY	E	•							•	•			Can be held to a neat 18 inches.
Chamaecyparis obtusa 'Nana' DWARF HINOKI CYPRESS	E	•						•	•	•	•		Very slow growing.
Choisya ternata MEXICAN ORANGE	E		•	•						•	•	•	Prefers light shade in all but cool-summer areas.
Cocculus laurifolius	E			•						•	•	•	Tolerates sun or shade, many soil types.
Cotoneaster horizontalis ROCK COTONEASTER	Semi E	•					•	•	•	•	•		Flat horizontal branches; widely used.
Hydrangea macrophylla BIGLEAF HYDRANGEA	D		•	•					•	•	•	•	Rounded plant with large bold leaves and thick flower clusters in white, blue, pink, or red.
Juniperus chinensis 'Armstrongii' ARMSTRONG JUNIPER	E	•					•	•	•	•	•		To 3 by 3 feet. More compact and smaller than Pfitzer juniper.
J. c. 'Blaauw' BLAAUW'S JUNIPER	E		•				•	•	•	•	•		Vase-shaped, about 4 feet high.
J. c. 'Fruitlandii' FRUITLAND JUNIPER	E		•				•	•	•	•	•		To 3 by 6 feet. Like a Pfitzer, but more compact.
J. c. 'Pfitzeriana' PFITZER JUNIPER	E			•		•	•	•	•	•	•	•	To 5 or 6 feet with arching branches to 12 feet or more.
J. horizontalis 'Plumosa' ANDORRA JUNIPER	E	•				•	•	•	•	•	•	•	To 18 inches, spreading to 10 feet. Plumy foliage. Plum color in winter.
J. sabina 'Tamariscifolia' TAMARIX JUNIPER, TAM	E	•					•	•	•	•	•	•	To 18 inches, wide spreading. Dense foliage.
Kalmia latifolia MOUNTAIN LAUREL	E		•	•		•	•	•	•	•	•	•	Needs acid soil. Glossy leathery leaves. Large clusters of pink and white flowers.
LANTANA	E	•	•	•							•	•	Many named hybrids differ in flower color and plant size.
Leucothoe fontanesiana DROOPING LEUCOTHOE	E		•					•	•	•	•		Needs acid soil. Good companion for rhododendrons, azaleas.
Mahonia aquifolium OREGON GRAPE	E	•	•					•	•	•	•		Leaves have spiny-toothed leaflets. Flowers in clusters; blue black edible fruits.
Nandina domestica HEAVENLY BAMBOO	E	•	•							•	•	•	Graceful foliage, red in fall and winter.
Pachistima canbyi CANBY PACHISTIMA	E	•				•	•	•	•				Requires acid soil and shade. Used for borders and low hedges.
Pernettya mucronata	E	•							•	•	•		Small dark green leaves give fine-textured look.
Philadelphus lemoinei	D			•		•	•	•	•				Many named varieties with single or double white flowers.
Pieris floribunda MOUNTAIN PIERIS	E	•	•				•	•	•	•	•		Needs acid soil. Blossoms in upright clusters.
Pinus mugo mughus MUGHO PINE	E	•	•		•	•	•	•	•	•			Slow growing. Shrubby, symmetrical.
Prunus ilicifolia HOLLYLEAF CHERRY	E			•						•	•	•	Must be trimmed to stay shrub size.
P. laurocerasus 'Zabeliana' ZABEL LAUREL	E		•						•	•	•	•	Branches angle upward and outward from base.
Raphiolepis indica INDIA HAWTHORN	E		•							•	•	•	Glossy dark green foliage. White to near red flowers.
RHODODENDRONS AND AZALEAS	D-E	•	•	•				•	•	•	•		See information on page 74.

Basic shrubs (cont'd.)

NAME OF PLANT	EVERGREEN OR DECIDUOUS	LESS THAN 3 FT.	3 TO 5 FT.	5 TO 8 FT.	CLIMATE ZONES								REMARKS
					3	4	5	6	7	8	9	10	
Rosmarinus officinalis ROSEMARY	E		●	●					●	●	●	●	Aromatic grayish foliage. Blue flowers. Prune to keep neat.
Sarcococca ruscifolia	E		●							●	●	●	Excellent for shade; polished deep green leaves and orderly growth.
Skimmia japonica	E		●							●	●		Slow growing, dense, broader than tall. Good in shady areas, under low windows.
Taxus baccata 'Repandens' SPREADING ENGLISH YEW	E	●					●	●	●	●			Dark green, needlelike foliage. Long horizontal branches.
Ternstroemia gymnanthera	E		●	●						●	●	●	New growth is bronzy red. Needs acid soil. Also good as a tub plant.
Viburnum burkwoodii	D			●				●	●	●	●		Pinkish white fragrant flowers. Almost evergreen in warm climates.
V. carlesii KOREAN SPICE VIBURNUM	D			●			●	●	●	●	●		Long grayish leaves. Pink buds open white.
V. davidii	E	●								●	●	●	Neat, compact dark green. Turquoise blue berries are an added dividend.
V. rhytidophyllum LEATHERLEAF VIBURNUM	E			●				●	●	●	●	●	Dark green, 7-inch leaves with wrinkled surface. Slow growing.

Rhododendrons

Areas where rhododendrons grow best have a cool and humid climate influenced by oceans or large lakes. In addition, winter low temperatures must remain above —25° F. for even the hardiest varieties. Considering these requirements, the most favorable rhododendron climates are found in coastal northern California, the Pacific Northwest west of the Cascades, and the area from Long Island to Philadelphia and south to Baltimore-Washington. Certain varieties will do well in two other favored territories: the Lake Erie shores of Ohio and Pennsylvania and from New York City north to Boston. In other areas of the country—wherever winter temperatures are not the limiting factor—the culture of rhododendrons is more difficult because of hot and humid summers (Atlantic and Gulf coast states) and hot, dry summers and alkaline soil (central and southern California).

The easiest to grow and those adapted to the widest range of climates are the Catawba hybrids—the "ironclad" group, all hardy to about —25°. These are the large-leafed, large-flowered, and fairly large-growing conventional hybrids that are at their best in woodland settings, in large borders, or massed in a bank planting. Some of the best in this group are 'Catawbiense Album' and 'Boule de Neige', both white; 'Mrs. C.S. Sargent' and 'Roseum Elegans', pink; and 'America', 'Caractacus', and 'Nova Zembla', red.

Slightly less hardy (to about —10°) are 'Cynthia', 'Mrs. Furnival', and 'Kate Waterer', dark pink; 'Dr. V.H. Rutgers' and 'Mars', red; 'Blue Peter', lavender blue; and 'Purple Splendour', dark purple.

Azaleas

Wherever they are adapted, azaleas can play important roles in woodland settings, shrub borders, mass displays, and foundation plantings. A vast array of hybrids are available, but most fall into the following categories of both evergreen and deciduous types:

Gable hybrids. Hardy in zone 5. Though classed as evergreen, the winter foliage is sparse. Most varieties are of medium height and are heavy flower producers.

Glenn Dale hybrids. A variable group of evergreens in both hardiness and growth habit, they are at their best in zones 6-9. Many varieties are available.

Knap Hill-Exbury hybrids. Hardy in zone 5. These have the largest flowers found in deciduous azaleas, and they are carried in magnificent clusters. Colors range from white through pink and yellow to orange and red.

Kurumes. These are most useful in zones 6-9. Handsome evergreen plants generally are low growing, compact, and densely foliaged with small leaves.

Macrantha hybrids. Included here are plants that are sometimes sold as Gumpo, Chugai, and Satsuki hybrids; hardiness is about the same as the Kurumes. Most Macranthas are very low growing and useful as ground covers or in edgings. All are late blooming.

Southern Indicas. These are the garden azaleas famous throughout the Deep South. They were selected for vigor and sun tolerance and may be sold as "sun azaleas." Most varieties take temperatures of 10° to 20°, but some are damaged even at 20°.

NAME OF PLANT	EVERGREEN OR DECIDUOUS	PERENNIAL	SHRUB	VINE	FLOWERS OR FRUIT	CLIMATE ZONES								REMARKS
						3	4	5	6	7	8	9	10	
Alyssum saxatile BASKET-OF-GOLD	E	•			•		•	•	•	•	•			Gray leaves, yellow flowers. May not survive cold winters.
Arctostaphylos uva-ursi BEARBERRY, KINNIKINNICK	E		•		•	•	•	•	•	•	•	•	•	White or pink flowers are followed by pink or red fruits.
Asparagus densiflorus 'Sprengeri' SPRENGER ASPARAGUS	E	•										•	•	Stems arch and droop to 6 feet if well grown.
BOUGAINVILLEA	E			•	•							•	•	One of the hardiest is sold under these names: San Diego Red, American Red, Scarlet O'Hara.
Campanula isophylla ITALIAN BELLFLOWER	E	•			•							•	•	Trailing or hanging stems to 2 feet long. Indoor-outdoor plant in cold areas.
Carissa grandiflora NATAL PLUM	E		•		•							•	•	Several named varieties are prostrate. Fruit is edible.
Ceanothus griseus horizontalis CARMEL CREEPER	E		•		•					•	•	•	•	Cut back any branches that grow upright.
Cistus salvifolius SAGELEAF ROCKROSE	E		•		•					•	•	•	•	Will take cold ocean winds, salt spray, or desert heat.
Cotoneaster adpressus CREEPING COTONEASTER	D		•		•		•	•	•	•	•	•		Slow growing, with ½-inch dark green leaves. Red fruit.
C. dammeri BEARBERRY COTONEASTER	E		•		•			•	•	•	•	•		Inch-long leaves on fast-growing plant. White flowers, red fruit.
C. horizontalis ROCK COTONEASTER	D		•		•			•	•	•	•			Will hang down 6 feet or more.
Euonymus fortunei 'Vegeta' BIG-LEAF WINTER CREEPER	E		•	•				•	•	•	•			Sends out long branches with side branches developing later.
Forsythia suspensa WEEPING FORSYTHIA	D		•		•			•	•	•	•			Drooping, vinelike branches.
Gelsemium sempervirens CAROLINA JESSAMINE	E			•	•							•	•	Long streamerlike branches cascade.
Hedera IVY	E			•				•	•	•	•	•	•	Grows down as well as up.
Iberis sempervirens EVERGREEN CANDYTUFT	E	•			•		•	•	•	•	•	•	•	For low walls.
Jasminum mesnyi PRIMROSE JASMINE	E			•	•						•	•	•	Large yellow flowers.
J. nudiflorum WINTER JASMINE	D			•	•				•	•	•	•		Slender willowy branches hang down.
Juniperus conferta SHORE JUNIPER	E		•						•	•	•	•		Will trail to 6 feet.
J. horizontalis 'Douglasii' WAUKEGAN JUNIPER	E		•			•	•	•	•	•	•	•		Trails to 8 feet.
Lotus berthelotii	E	•			•						•	•	•	Scarlet flowers stand out against feathery, silver gray leaves.
Pelargonium peltatum IVY GERANIUM	E	•			•							•	•	Many varieties with bright, showy flowers. Light green, ivylike leaves.
Rosmarinus officinalis 'Prostratus' DWARF ROSEMARY	E		•		•						•	•	•	Endures hot sun and poor soil. Cascading branches will make a green curtain.
Sollya fusiformis AUSTRALIAN BLUEBELL CREEPER	E		•		•						•	•	•	Clusters of brilliant blue, bell-shaped flowers appear in summer.
Trachelospermum jasminoides STAR JASMINE	E			•	•					•	•	•	•	Glossy, 3-inch leaves and powerfully fragrant white flowers.
Vinca minor DWARF PERIWINKLE	E			•	•		•	•	•	•	•	•	•	Long trailing stems hang down.

NAME OF PLANT	EVERGREEN OR DECIDUOUS	AREA LESS THAN 500 SQ. FT.	AREA MORE THAN 500 SQ. FT.	SUN	SHADE	CLIMATE ZONES								REMARKS
						3	4	5	6	7	8	9	10	
Ajuga reptans	E	•	•	•	•		•	•	•	•	•	•	•	Choice. Widely adapted.
Anthemis nobilis CHAMOMILE	E	•	•	•	•			•	•	•	•	•	•	Green carpet.
Arctostaphylos uva-ursi BEARBERRY, KINNIKINNICK	E	•	•	•	•	•	•	•	•	•	•			Prostrate, spreading and rooting as it creeps. Requires acid soil.
Ardisia japonica	E	•	•		•					•	•	•	•	Spreads by rhizomes. Leathery bright green leaves. White flowers in fall. Bright red fruits. Suggests holly.
Carissa grandiflora 'Tuttle' NATAL PLUM	E	•		•								•	•	Grows to 2 feet high, spreading 5 feet wide. Dark green glossy leaves. White flowers. Edible red fruits.
Cerastium tomentosum SNOW-IN-SUMMER	E	•		•			•	•	•	•	•	•		Spreading dense tufty mats of silvery gray. Snow white masses of flowers in early summer.
Cotoneaster conspicuus 'Decorus' NECKLACE COTONEASTER	E	•		•					•	•	•	•	•	Low spreading.
C. dammeri BEARBERRY COTONEASTER	E	•	•	•					•	•	•	•	•	Flat, long trailing branches.
C. horizontalis ROCK COTONEASTER	D	•		•					•	•	•	•	•	Mounding.
C. 'Lowfast'	E	•	•	•										Thick, low, neat.
Euonymus fortunei radicans COMMON WINTER CREEPER	E		•	•	•			•	•	•	•	•		*E. f.* 'Colorata' has same spreading growth but leaves turn dark purple in winter.
Gaultheria procumbens WINTERGREEN, CHECKERBERRY	E	•	•		•	•	•	•	•	•	•	•		Acid soil. Naturalistic planting.
Hedera helix ENGLISH IVY	E	•	•	•	•			•	•	•	•	•	•	Many varieties sold. Needs winter protection in zone 5.
H. h. 'Baltica' BALTIC IVY	E	•	•	•	•			•	•	•	•	•	•	Hardier than above.
H. h. 'Hahn's self-branching' HAHN'S SELF-BRANCHING IVY	E	•		•	•				•	•	•	•	•	Small areas, planters.
Hypericum calycinum AARON'S BEARD	Semi E		•	•	•			•	•	•	•	•	•	Rugged grower.
Iberis sempervirens EVERGREEN CANDYTUFT	E	•		•				•	•	•	•	•	•	Small areas, edgings.
IRISH MOSS, SCOTCH MOSS	E	•		•	•			•	•	•	•	•		Green and yellow green carpets.
Juniperus chinensis sargentii SARGENT JUNIPER	E	•	•	•			•	•	•	•	•	•	•	Steel blue, ground-hugging.
J. conferta SHORE JUNIPER	E	•	•	•				•	•	•	•	•	•	Light green. Good at seashore.
J. horizontalis CREEPING JUNIPER	E	•	•	•		•	•	•	•	•	•	•	•	Forms blue gray mat 18 inches high.
J. h. 'Bar Harbor' BAR HARBOR JUNIPER	E	•	•	•			•	•	•	•	•	•	•	Plum color in winter.
J. h. 'Douglasii' WAUKEGAN JUNIPER	E	•	•	•		•	•	•	•	•	•	•	•	Turns purple in fall.
J. h. 'Plumosa' ANDORRA JUNIPER	E	•	•	•			•	•	•	•	•	•	•	Feathery. Plum color in cold winter.
J. sabina 'Tamariscifolia' TAM JUNIPER	E	•	•	•				•	•	•	•	•	•	Favorite in warm areas.

Ground Covers

NAME OF PLANT	EVERGREEN OR DECIDUOUS	AREA LESS THAN 500 SQ. FT.	AREA MORE THAN 500 SQ. FT.	SUN	SHADE	CLIMATE ZONES								REMARKS
						3	4	5	6	7	8	9	10	
Liriope muscari BIG BLUE LILY TURF	E	●		●	●				●	●	●	●	●	Grasslike leaves; blue flowers.
Lonicera japonica 'Halliana' HALL'S HONEYSUCKLE	E		●	●				●	●	●	●	●	●	Good in tough situations. Invasive.
Ophiopogon japonicus MONDO GRASS	E	●	●	●	●					●	●	●	●	A variegated form is available. Widely used zones 9, 10.
Pachysandra terminalis	E	●	●		●			●	●	●	●			Best in acid soil. Valuable ground cover in shade and semishade.
Phlox subulata MOSS PINK	E	●		●		●	●	●	●	●	●	●		Late spring and summer color in a 6-inch-deep carpet.
Rosa wichuraiana MEMORIAL ROSE	D	●	●	●					●	●	●	●	●	Good for dry banks, rocky slopes.
Rosmarinus officinalis 'Prostratus' DWARF ROSEMARY	E	●		●						●	●	●	●	Spreads 4 to 8 feet. Stays less than 2 feet high.
Trachelospermum jasminoides STAR JASMINE	E		●	●	●					●	●	●	●	Fragrant. Cut back to keep low.
Vinca minor DWARF PERIWINKLE	E	●	●	●	●		●	●	●	●	●	●	●	Widely used.

Vines

NAME OF PLANT	EVERGREEN OR DECIDUOUS	FLOWERS	DISTINCTIVE FOLIAGE	ATTRACTIVE FRUIT	CLINGS	NEEDS TYING	CLIMATE ZONES								REMARKS
							3	4	5	6	7	8	9	10	
Actinidia chinensis KIWI VINE, CHINESE GOOSEBERRY	D	●	●	●		●					●	●	●	●	Delicious edible fruit if male and female plants are grown together.
Ampelopsis brevipedunculata BLUEBERRY CLIMBER	D			●	●				●	●	●	●	●	●	Brilliant metallic blue berries in late summer and fall.
Beaumontia grandiflora HERALD'S TRUMPET, EASTER LILY VINE	E	●	●			●							●	●	Needs rich soil, ample water, heavy fertilizing. Easter lilylike flowers.
BOUGAINVILLEA	E	●				●							●	●	Where frost occurs, give plants the warmest spot in the garden.
Campsis radicans COMMON TRUMPET CREEPER	D	●			●				●	●	●	●	●		Rampant growth, needs periodic thinning. Flowers grow in clusters.
Cissus antarctica KANGAROO TREEBINE	E		●		●								●	●	Vigorous but restrained growth.
C. rhombifolia GRAPE IVY	E		●		●								●	●	Grows well in sun or shade.
Clematis armandii EVERGREEN CLEMATIS	E	●				●					●	●	●	●	Needs constant pruning after flowering to prevent buildup of dead thatch.
C. jackmanii	D	●				●				●	●	●	●	●	Many hybrids with large showy flowers.
C. montana ANEMONE CLEMATIS	D	●				●				●	●	●	●	●	Vigorous and easy to grow. Massive spring flower display.

NAME OF PLANT	EVERGREEN OR DECIDUOUS	FLOWERS	DISTINCTIVE FOLIAGE	ATTRACTIVE FRUIT	CLINGS	NEEDS TYING	CLIMATE ZONES								REMARKS
							3	4	5	6	7	8	9	10	
Clytostoma callistegioides VIOLET TRUMPET VINE	E	•	•			•						•	•	•	Sun or shade. Needs pruning after flowering to prevent tangling.
Euonymus fortunei radicans COMMON WINTER CREEPER	E		•	•					•	•	•	•			One of best broad-leafed evergreen vines where temperatures drop below 0°.
Fatshedera lizei	E		•			•						•	•	•	Highly polished 6 to 8-inch leaves look like giant ivy.
Ficus pumila CREEPING FIG	E		•	•									•	•	Rampant growth. Juvenile leaves are tiny and delicate; mature growth has large, leathery foliage.
Gelsemium sempervirens CAROLINA JESSAMINE	E	•	•			•							•	•	Vigorous but neat. Foliage pattern is not dense.
GRAPE	D		•	•		•									Bold foliage pattern. Adaptability varies according to variety.
Hardenbergia comptoniana LILAC VINE	E	•				•							•	•	Delicate foliage pattern, striking clusters of violet blue flowers.
Hedera canariensis ALGERIAN IVY	E		•		•							•	•		Makes a dense cover. There is also a form with white and green leaves.
H. helix ENGLISH IVY	E		•		•					•	•	•	•	•	Will completely cover whatever it climbs on.
Hibbertia scandens GUINEA GOLD VINE	E	•				•							•	•	Restrained climber. Yellow flowers resemble single roses.
Hydrangea anomala petiolaris CLIMBING HYDRANGEA	D	•	•		•				•	•	•	•	•		Shrubby and sprawling without a support to cling to.
Jasminum grandiflorum SPANISH JASMINE	D or Semi E	•	•			•							•	•	Open growth gives airy effect. Fragrant flowers all summer.
J. nitidum ANGELWING JASMINE	E or Semi E	•	•			•								•	Not reliably hardy below 25°.
J. polyanthum	E	•	•			•							•	•	Strong growing and fast climbing.
Kadsura japonica SCARLET KADSURA	E		•	•		•						•	•		Fall and winter color comes from clusters of scarlet fruit.
Lonicera hildebrandiana GIANT BURMESE HONEYSUCKLE	E	•				•							•	•	Bold and heavy-textured with a semi-tropical appearance.
L. japonica JAPANESE HONEYSUCKLE	E	•				•			•	•	•	•	•	•	Rank growth needs control. Will form solid screen if grown on chain link fence.
Mandevilla laxa CHILEAN JASMINE	D	•	•										•	•	White, trumpet-shaped flowers have strong gardenia fragrance.
Parthenocissus quinquefolia VIRGINIA CREEPER	D		•	•	•		•	•	•	•	•	•	•	•	Clings to vertical surfaces or will double as ground cover. Good fall color.
P. tricuspidata BOSTON IVY	D		•	•	•				•	•	•	•	•	•	The ivy of the "Ivy League." Makes a fast, dense, even wall cover. Good fall color.
Passiflora alato-caerulea PASSION VINE	E	•	•	•								•	•	•	Striking, unusual flowers are white, lavender, and purple.
Phaedranthus buccinatorius BLOOD-RED TRUMPET VINE	E	•	•	•									•	•	Red flowers come in bursts throughout the year whenever weather warms.

NAME OF PLANT	EVERGREEN OR DECIDUOUS	FLOWERS	DISTINCTIVE FOLIAGE	ATTRACTIVE FRUIT	CLINGS	NEEDS TYING	CLIMATE ZONES								REMARKS
							3	4	5	6	7	8	9	10	
Polygonum aubertii SILVER LACE VINE	D-E	●	●		●				●	●	●	●	●	●	Very rapid growth, but can be pruned to the ground yearly if necessary.
Rhoicissus capensis EVERGREEN GRAPE	E		●	●									●	●	Will grow in full sun but roots need shade.
ROSE (climbing)	D-E	●		●											Many named varieties in various colors and flower sizes.
Tetrastigma voinierianum	E		●	●									●	●	Good eave-line decoration. Glossy, dark green leaves may reach 1 foot across.
WISTERIA	D	●	●		●				●	●	●	●	●	●	Showy, pendant flower clusters. Plants need careful, early training.

For quick color... annuals and perennials

Once you've selected trees, shrubs, vines, ground covers and other materials to form your permanent planting framework, you'll want to fill in with colorful plants that last for one season or longer.

To add color to your garden, choose from among the following annuals or perennials:

Easy-to-Grow

Achillea
Aquilegia
Arctotis
Balsam
Bells of Ireland
Calendula
Celosia
Cleome
Cosmos
Dahlia
Daisy
Dianthus
Digitalis
Gaillardia
Gomphrena
Gypsophila
Hemerocallis
Hollyhock
Larkspur
Marigold
Nasturtium
Nigella
Pansy
Phlox
Portulaca
Scabiosa
Sedum
Shasta Daisy
Strawflower
Sweet Pea
Tritoma
Zinnia

Small Edging and Dwarf Beds

Ageratum
Alyssum
Aster
Brachycome
Browallia
Calliopsis
Celosia
Coleus
Dahlia
Dianthus
Dimorphotheca
Impatiens
Marigold
Mimulus
Myosotis
Nasturtium
Nierembergia
Pansy
Petunia
Phlox
Portulaca
Salvia
Snapdragon
Torenia
Verbena
Vinca

Background and Tall Beds

Achillea
Amaranthus
Anthemis
Campanula
Celosia
Centaurea
Chrysanthemum
Cynoglossum
Datura
Delphinium
Dusty Miller
Gaillardia
Gloriosa Daisy
Heliopsis
Hemerocallis
Iris
Lily
Lupine
Marigold
Nicotiana
Phlox
Pyrethrum
Rudbeckia
Salvia
Scabiosa
Shasta Daisy
Snapdragon
Sweet William
Tritoma

Fragrance

Carnation
Centaurea moschata
Dianthus plumarius
Freesia
Gardenia
Lavender
Lilium
Stock
Sweet Pea
Sweet William
Viola odorata

Moist Situations

Anenome
Aquilegia
Boltonia
Browallia
Caladium
Hemerocallis
Hibiscus
Iris kaempferi
Linaria cymbalaria
Lobelia cardinalis
Lupine
Lythrum
Mignonette
Monarda
Myosotis
Physostegia
Ranunculus
Tradescantia
Trollius
Viola

Dry Areas

Achillea
Arctotis
Armeria
Brachycome
Cactus
Calliopsis
Catananche
Centaurea
Coreopsis
Dianthus
Echium
Eschscholzia
Euphorbia
Gaillardia
Geranium
Gypsophila
Helianthus
Hollyhock
Ice Plant
Lathyrus latifolius
Nasturtium
Oenothera
Penstemon
Portulaca
Rudbeckia
Scabiosa
Sedum
Sempervivum
Yucca

Partial Shade

Aconitum
Alyssum
Anchusa
Anemone
Aquilegia
Astilbe
Azalea
Begonia
Blackberry Lily
Centaurea
Clematis
Coleus
Coreopsis
Cyclamen
Digitalis
Doronicum
Ferns
Helleborus
Hemerocallis
Hypericum
Impatiens
Iris
Liriope
Lobelia
Lythrum
Mignonette
Mimulus
Myosotis
Nierembergia
Physostegia
Polemonium
Primrose
Ranunculus
Saxifraga
Thalictrum
Torenia
Tradescantia
Viola

Cutting

Achillea
Ageratum
Anemone
Anthemis
Aquilegia
Calliopsis
Candytuft
Carnation
Centaurea
China Aster
Chrysanthemum
Clarkia
Coreopsis
Cynoglossum
Delphinium
Dianthus
Didiscus
Gerbera
Gloriosa Daisy
Gypsophila
Helianthus
Helichrysum
Heliopsis
Lathyrus
Marigold
Mignonette
Myosotis
Pyrethrum
Rudbeckia
Salpiglossis
Shasta Daisy
Snapdragon
Stock
Sweet William
Tithonia
Veronica
Wallflower

Index

Photographers

Robert G. Bander: 7 top right; 57 bottom; 59 bottom; back cover, top.
Glenn Christiansen: 2 top; 32; 59 top. **Richard Fish:** 2 bottom; 3 top; 4-5; 6 top right; 7 middle left; 25; 29 top; 52 top; 60 middle left and right; 60 bottom; 62 top; 62 bottom right; 64. **Steve Marley:** 50-51. **Ells Marugg:** 3 bottom; 6 top left; 6 bottom right; 7 middle right; 7 bottom; 28 top; 29 bottom left and right; 56 bottom; 57 middle; 58 top left; 60 top; 62 bottom left; back cover, middle and bottom. **Bill Ross:** 3 top; 4 inset; 6 bottom left; 7 top left; 30 inset; 30-31; 50 inset; 56 top. **Darrow M. Watt:** 58 top right. **Stephen Wells:** 28 bottom; 58 bottom.